COASTAL CONNECTICUT

Eastern Region

Coastal Connecticut

Eastern Region

By Barry and Susan Hildebrandt

Peregrine Press

Box 751 Old Saybrook, Conn. 06475

Cover: A foggy morning at Mystic Seaport
Photograph by Oliver Denison III

Designed by Ann S. Haslam
Calligraphy by Michael Alan Fox

Manufactured in the United States of America

First Printing

ISBN O-933614-00-4

Table of contents

Introduction	3
Stonington	7
Mystic	13
Groton	27
New London	35
Waterford	45
East Lyme	51
Old Lyme	57
Lyme	63
East Haddam	67
Chester	73
Deep River	77
Essex	79
Old Saybrook	87
Westbrook	93
Clinton	95
Killingworth	99
Madison	101
Guilford	107
Index	113

Acknowledgements

Any project of this kind cannot be accomplished without the help of literally hundreds of people. We would like to thank the various state agencies, historical societies, town governments, and Chambers of Commerce for their wholehearted cooperation and enthusiasm. Special thanks must go to those persons who went out of their way to give us private tours of closed-up museums, and to those restauranteurs who gave us a warm welcome. Particular thanks must go to Ruth Hildebrandt for her much-needed help in proofreading, and to Florence Hildebrandt, whose correcting of the galley proofs was done in what has to be world record time. And finally, we are indebted to Nancy Haslam and Michael Fox, without whose enormous talents (and love of good food) this book would never have become a reality. Despite the assistance and cooperation of all these wonderful people, there may be some errors or omissions; for these, we assume full responsibility.

Introduction

There's an old saw that says that Connecticut's sights and attractions are among the state's best kept secrets, and this is partially true. Mystic Seaport, of course, is known all over the world, and from time to time some event (the Blessing of the Fleet, the Fife and Drum Muster, etc.) hits the regional or national news and attracts some interest. But what is generally not known is that this beautiful and historic state, in particular its eastern coastal region, teems with fascinating places for a family or an individual to visit and enjoy. Connecticut has always been considered a state that a tourist has to pass through to get from one place to another, and that's a mistake: there's too much here to ignore.

Any tourist (indeed, any resident) with a few days' free time in any area always seeks the interesting, the unique, or the fun thing to do. When we first moved to Connecticut, those were our aims, but we were considerably frustrated to find that there was no central listing, no non-commercial descriptive material, no book, nothing at all that could give us the information we needed to explore the area, learn about it, and get the most from it. We compiled this guide in the course of our own explorations of the region, and studies about its history. We discovered a multitude of fascinating things to see and do, all included in this book.

Although Connecticut is the third smallest state in the nation, it is as rich in history and tradition as any. The eastern coastal region, first settled only a few years after Plymouth, has had and continues to have a dramatic and colorful role in the development of the United States. Its towns have defended themselves against Indian raids, British invasion, the ravages of nature, and a radically changing American society. They have given the country judges, generals, legislators, explorers, inventors, educators, and heroes. They have tried their hand at every conceivable industry, and today the world's largest manufacturers of such diverse commodities as witch hazel, piano keys, and nuclear submarines are located in this region. Bordering the sea, these towns have played a major part in America's seafaring history, both militarily and commercially. Vessels from just about every port on the shore took part in whaling expeditions, blockade running, the West Indies and China trade, voyages of exploration, and privateering raids. The rocky New England soil is poorly suited to agriculture, so when the expansion westward began, farmers from these towns were among the first to settle Pennsylvania, Ohio, Indiana, and Illinois, and many of them gave their names to cities and towns in that area. Part of the charm of the eastern coastal region is its history and its reaction to change. What a place was in the past has an important effect on what it is in the present, and for this reason, a brief historical sketch of each town has been included.

Yankee ingenuity and stubbornness also played a part in these histories. The early pioneers, trying to carve a life out of the wilderness and the sea, came up with ideas, methods, contraptions, and products that were unheard of before. They were inventive geniuses and true entrepreneurs. They were also tough. Deacon Phineas Pratt of Deep River, shortly after the Revolution, advertised that he was "the inventor and maker of any machinery that would enable the manufacturer to compete with the British." This self-confidence and temerity is doubtless what has contributed to the so-called "American spirit," and the reason that this country has become what it is today.

The countryside and the shore of this region are truly lovely. Rolling hills, rushing brooks, thick forests, and an alternating rocky and sandy coast combine to make this area one of the prettiest in New England. America's last unspoiled Great River, the magnificent Connecticut, divides the region. We have pointed out various drives, walks, and viewpoints where the traveler may enjoy some of this beauty.

4

Some notes on this book:

How to use this guide — This guide is laid out by town, starting with Stonington at the Rhode Island border and proceeding towards New Haven. Each town is divided into three sections: a historical sketch, things to see and do, and dining recommendations. Most of the 18 towns included in this book have smaller villages and communities within their borders (for example, Niantic, Moodus, Ivoryton, and Noank). These may be located by referring to the index at the back of the book. References to sights, attractions, and restaurants may be found there as well. We have not included any maps, as any standard road map will get you close enough to follow the detailed written directions to each place.

Prices and hours — All prices and hours listed in this book were in effect at presstime, and are, of course, subject to change. The prices and hours for various attractions and museums will change little, if any, before this guide is updated. The restaurant prices, however, are bound to go up, and the reader is cautioned that the prices quoted in this book are guidelines only, and are meant to give the reader an idea of the various selections available and their *approximate* price ranges.

Restaurants — We have visited just about every restaurant of note in the region, and from these have selected a group of 30 that we consider the best. We could have written a bite-by-bite review of the meals we've eaten, but we feel such reviews are silly, boring, and irrelevant. Rather, we have chosen to try to give the reader a general description of the restaurant and the various types of dishes available along with their approximate prices. When an establishment has one or more dishes that are very special or popular, we've pointed these out as a further help to those searching out a good meal. A star (★) has been awarded to our personal favorites: places we would recommend without hesitation to anyone.

Directions — Traveling the coast of Connecticut without a compass can be very confusing. Nine out of ten people feel that when they are driving from New York to Boston they are heading due north. Not true, especially along the Connecticut shore where the direction is east-west. (Just head towards New York at sundown and you'll see what we mean.)

Pay no attention to the I-95 entrance signs: they use north and east, or south and west as synonymous, changing arbitrarily from sign to sign. Just remember that south is towards Long Island Sound, east is towards Providence and Boston, and west is towards New Haven and New York.

So take your time — explore this fascinating region and see what life was like 300 years ago and what it is today. You'll never forget it, and undoubtedly will return again and again. Or, like us, you may choose to settle in this peaceful and wonderful place. In any event, enjoy, enjoy!

Barry and Susan Hildebrandt
March, 1979

Stonington

Stonington (so named because of its rocky soil), more than most towns along Long Island Sound, has kept its seafaring atmosphere almost intact. Surrounded on three sides by water, Stonington Borough (the population center) has always been associated with the sea and the commerce related to it. Even today, the town serves as the home port for the last significant fishing fleet in Connecticut, and the beautiful harbor is a popular haven for pleasure boats.

The area around Stonington played a major part in the Indian Wars during the 1630s and for a while the region was claimed by both the Connecticut Colony and the Massachusetts Bay Colony. Stonington Borough, occupying a finger of land jutting into the Sound, was laid out as a town in 1752 and incorporated in 1801. The strategic importance of the town was recognized by the British during the War of 1812: if they controlled Stonington, they could control the eastern entrance to Long Island Sound. Early in August, 1814, five British ships anchored offshore and for three days lobbed cannonballs into the town. Refusing to surrender, the townspeople fought back and, with the help of two 18-pound cannons, succeeded in severely damaging one of the frigates, causing the British to withdraw. Thus the Battle of Stonington was fought and another chapter in American stubbornness and bravery was written.

Until the advent of steam-powered ships, Stonington was one of the busiest ports on the coast. Shipbuilding was the major industry here for almost 200 years, and, despite its small size, Stonington was a major whaling port. A sizeable Portu-

7

guese population in the town today is largely composed of descendants of crewmen picked up on whaling expeditions to the Azores in the 1830s.

Many notable seamen called Stonington home, the most famous of which was Capt. Nathaniel Palmer. In 1821, at the age of 21, while on a sealing expedition off South America, Palmer discovered the Antarctic continent, which today has a sizeable piece of land named after him. In later years, he became a builder and skipper of clipper ships; on one voyage he set the 84-day record for the New York to Hong Kong run. Another resident who achieved fame at an early age was Edmund Fanning, who, at the age of 18, discovered the Fanning Islands, 1000 miles south of Hawaii. Not all the residents were seafaring folk, however: James Whistler and Stephen Vincent Benét lived here too. Now a haven for retirees, this charming town presently lists a number of nationally-known figures on its voting roles.

The section of Mystic east of the Mystic River is a part of Stonington, but for purposes of this guide, that area has been treated separately.

Things to see & do

Stonington Borough is a quaint and delightful coastal village faintly reminiscent of Marblehead and Nantucket, and is well worth the trip. The Stonington Historical Society has produced a very good and very detailed walking map of the village which may be picked up at the Old Lighthouse Museum. If you don't have time for a walk, don't leave town without taking a drive up Main Street north from Cannon Square where there are many well-preserved homes of the eighteenth and nineteenth centuries, displaying a wide variety of architectural styles. The unique 16-star, 16-stripe flag that flew during the Battle of Stonington is on display in the bank adjacent to Cannon Square. And be sure to drive down to the point at the foot of Water Street where there are amazing views of Fishers Island and Little Narragansett Bay. The imposing fort-like structure on Pearl Street looks as if it were designed and situated to repel the British fleet, but it fights more prosaic battles: it's the local water treatment plant.

8

Old Lighthouse Museum — Originally built in 1823, this was the earliest U.S. Government-sponsored lighthouse in Connecticut. Erosion of the shore threatened the structure, so in 1840 it was taken apart stone by stone and moved to its present location, where it operated for many years. The building was acquired by the Stonington Historical Society in 1910 and became a museum in 1925.

This fine small museum devotes itself to displays concerned with the early history of the town. Along with other relics of the Battle of Stonington, there's an extensive collection of cannonballs which landed on the town during the battle, including one that became imbedded in a hearth. Some of the town's early industries, including shipbuilding, pottery, firearms manufacturing, and ice harvesting are represented by well-designed and colorful displays. In addition, there are portraits of the early settlers, farm implements, navigation instruments, antique dolls, relics of the China trade, and whaling paraphernalia. This is a very complete and well-done museum that is worth a stop. The building itself is interesting, and the view from the grounds is breathtaking.

The Old Lighthouse Museum is located on the point at the foot of Water Street. It is open during the summer months, daily except Monday, from 11 a.m. to 4:30 p.m. Admission is 75¢ for adults and 25¢ for children 6 to 12.

Photo Courtesy of Connecticut Department of Commerce

Old Lighthouse Museum

9

Pullman Museum — Yes, you might say that Jim Bradley is a real train buff. He took his life savings and, instead of buying a condominium in Florida, he shot the whole works on six Pullman cars which sit, finally at rest, in his back yard. (The story of how they got there is another trip in itself.) Mr. Bradley believes that the days of plush rail travel are gone forever and has done what other concerned people might be too timid to do: he has purchased and is lovingly restoring old one-of-a-kind railroad cars in hopes of preserving them forever.

The parlor car, with swiveling wing-back armchairs, dates from 1930, and was once the pride of "The Yankee Clipper." The coaches, now beautifully restored, date from as far back as 1914. But the real treat is the sleeper, complete with staterooms, fold-down beds, and chair toilets. A wonderful view of the Sound can be enjoyed from the observation platform of the "schoolroom car." Mr. Bradley will take you through each car and describe its history and function.

To get there, take Williams Street (in Stonington Borough) east for about two-tenths of a mile; bear left on Elm Street and turn right at Bayview Avenue; wind around behind the American Velvet factory and turn right on Cheeseboro Road. The museum is at the end of the road. There are no regular hours, but Mr. Bradley is willing to share his hobby anytime. To make sure he's there, call 203-535-1021 ahead of time. Admission is free, but donations are appreciated.

Blessing of the Fleet — On the second Sunday of each July, ten to fifteen thousand people descend on the tiny town of Stonington to witness the Blessing of the Fleet, an event inspired by ancient European custom. On the Saturday evening preceding the blessing, there are block parties, clambakes, and dances. On Sunday morning at 9 a.m., a high mass is celebrated at St. Mary's Church followed by an hour-long parade at 1 p.m. After this, the boats parade by in the harbor, each to be blessed by the Bishop. The vessels, mostly from the Stonington fishing fleet, are gaily decorated, and a prize is awarded for the most lavishly-adorned boat. This is a wild, fun day, but it is not without its solemn aspects: many of the ceremonies are concerned with prayers and dedications to those men of Stonington who never returned from the sea. In case of rain or for further information, call 203-535-1700.

Dining

★**Harborview** — In New England, when you hear of a restaurant named Harborview, you immediately think "well, another fish house." This particular establishment should be called Chez Lucien or Maison Pierre or La Plume de Ma Tante, for at Harborview you will feast on absolutely outstanding French food. Be sure to give this restaurant a try, but take a full wallet: it's very expensive (and always worth it). In a dimly lighted Victorian setting, the diners, many of whom have traveled a long distance to eat here, enjoy an excellent meal. The place is usually crowded and a bit noisy, but it is worth almost anything you might endure.

Before you order any of a nice selection of fairly expensive appetizers, be aware that the helpings on the entrees are enormous. The menu is exclusively classic French and includes a variety of meat dishes, several poultry dishes, and excellent selections of veal and seafood. Everything on the menu is superb, especially the veal, but the Caneton au Muscadet (duckling with white onions, grapes, and walnuts) and the Sole Marguery (poached sole sauced with shrimp, mushrooms, and mussels) could win every award in the book. The wine list is fairly narrow, but there's something here you'll like at a moderate price. For the few who still have room, desserts are available.

At luncheon, you can enjoy excellent French entrees including fish, meat, and egg dishes at $4.95 to $7.50. Appetizers and salads are the same as on the dinner menu at the same prices. In the bar, a super blackboard lunch, consisting of sandwiches, fish and chips, and salads, is available at much lower prices.

The Harborview Restaurant is located on Water Street in downtown Stonington Borough, about one-half mile from the point, and adjacent to Cannon Square. Luncheon is served from 11:45 a.m. to 3 p.m. daily except Tuesday. Dinner is served from 5 p.m. to 10 p.m. except on Sunday when the hours are 4 p.m. to 9 p.m. The restaurant is closed on Tuesdays. Reservations are a must. Credit cards: AE, BA/V, DC, MC. 203-535-2720.

Stonington

Sandy's — What was once a fish and lobster shack among the Stonington wharves is now a popular eatery where you can enjoy the best of the harvest from New England waters at an unbelievably low price. Like Abbott's in Noank, Sandy's is a no-frills restaurant where you go to enjoy the view, be as messy as you want to be, and fill up on beautifully-cooked seafood. You have your choice of eating at picnic tables either inside or outside; in either place, wonderful views of Stonington harbor, Fishers Island Sound, and all the summer boating traffic are right there.

Just go to the counter and place your order for lobster (single or twin), crabs, or fresh fish (flounder, scallops, swordfish, etc.), and then off to the clam bar for raw clams, steamers, or a superior clam chowder. Eventually (the wait, really, is pretty short), you'll be called and you can sit down and gorge yourself. Cole slaw and potato chips come with the meal, and corn-on-the-cob is available too. The prices, which vary with the catch, are as low as you'll find in the region. Coffee and soft drinks may be purchased, but if you want anything stronger, bring your own. Sandy says, "eat fish—live longer," and judging from the popularity of this place, there's going to be a lot of octogenarians around. A retail store on the premises sells lobsters and fresh fish.

Sandy's is located off Water Street in Stonington Borough directly behind the Harborview Restaurant. It is open only during the summer, from about Memorial Day to about Labor Day. Meals are served from 5 p.m. to 9 p.m. on weekdays, and from noon to 10 p.m. on Saturday and Sunday. Sandy's does not accept reservations or credit cards. 203-535-3018.

Mystic

Despite the fact that Mystic is the most popular tourist town in Connecticut, it really is not a town at all. Rather, it is a part of two other towns: Groton claims the section of Mystic west of the Mystic River, while the eastern section is a part of Stonington.

Mystic shares with many other towns a long history in shipbuilding, shipping and whaling, but its accomplishments in these endeavors are far out of proportion to its size. The first settlers of the area, in the 1600s, were farmers in the summer and shipbuilders in the winter. The call of the sea gradually took precedence, and by the end of the eighteenth century, Mystic harbor was a bustling port, with the shore lined with shipyards and riggers. Between 1822 and 1850, shipbuilding and particularly whaling were the major industries. In the mid-1840s, there were 18 whaleships sailing out of Mystic, a remarkable figure when you realize that the population of the town at that time was a mere 1500. By the end of that decade, with the rush to California in full swing, Mystic shipbuilders turned their attention to building clipper ships. These Mystic-built vessels were big and sleek and had a reputation for being among the fastest in the world. Indeed, some of them established records that have never been broken.

By the Civil War, the shipbuilders, always ready to change with the times, were turning out steamships; by the end of the nineteenth century, large sailing yachts were being produced. After 1920, shipbuilding as a major industry began to decline, and the Mystic yards produced a trickle of yachts and fishing

13

Mystic

vessels, though during World War II there was quite a flurry of small craft contracts from the U.S. Navy and the Coast Guard.

Mystic is an old, graceful town with a dramatic history linked to the sea. It is appropriate that the finest maritime museum in the nation, and perhaps the world, is located here.

Things to see & do

Mystic Seaport Maritime Museum — Mystic Seaport is probably the most famous maritime museum in the world, and annually plays host to more than half a million visitors. This is an organization dedicated to America's maritime heritage, and what was a one-building exhibit in 1929 has today become a 40-acre complex with more than 60 buildings. It is fitting that the museum is located on the site of the old Greenman shipyard, one of the most prolific shipbuilders in the area. Between 1838 and 1878, Greenman's launched more than 100 ships, including the famous clipper *David Crockett,* whose average performance on 25 runs around Cape Horn to San Francisco was never equaled.

Photo by Kenneth E. Mahler

Mystic Seaport In Winter

This is very much a working museum, with the public invited to observe the restoration efforts, crafts manufacturing, shipbuilding, and other activities. The addition to the museum's collection is ongoing, and there's always some kind of work taking place. Buildings have been brought here from all over the East, and there is a constant search for new and unique exhibits that exemplify New England's shipping, shipbuilding, and fisheries heritage.

Visitors should allow at least one full day to explore and enjoy Mystic Seaport. There are interesting things everywhere, and it's not hard to become so caught up in one exhibit that half the day is gone before you know it. So, allow plenty of time to see everything.

Some of the highlights:

Probably the most famous exhibit of the museum is the *Charles W. Morgan,* the last of the wooden whaleships. Built in New Bedford in 1841, she continued whaling until 1921. The *Morgan* was acquired by the museum in 1941. Dominating the wharf, this graceful vessel is one of the most photographed ships in America. The working and living spaces have been fully restored, and things are so real that, going aboard, you'll be looking over your shoulder for Capt. Ahab and his cohorts.

Other floating exhibits include the *L. A. Dunton,* a rare 123-foot Gloucester fisherman, one of the ablest and fastest fishing vessels ever built, the 103-foot square-rigged training ship *Joseph Conrad,* and various smaller smacks, cutters, and sloops, all of historic interest.

An enormous collection of small boats, the largest such group in the United States, can be found in various sheds. Numbering more than 200 sail, power, and rowing-type boats, the collection includes everything from rowboats to yachts. As an example of the depth of this exhibit, there are more than two dozen different types of canoes displayed.

Other buildings contain many of the crafts and industries that went to support shipping and shipbuilding. There's a sail loft, a ropewalk, a chandlery, a shipsmith, a coopery, and a hoop shop, most with working craftsmen keeping alive the old skills and willing to answer any questions.

There are old houses filled with antiques and homes honoring famous sailing families. There are buildings with ship models, figureheads, clocks, folk arts and fine arts, oystering memorabilia, and everything else you can imagine. Laid out like a small village, the Seaport has a general store, a drug store, a chapel, and a school. There's even a planetarium. A children's museum is especially good and should not be missed by the youngsters.

Special events and programs are held year-round. There are films and lectures, sea chantey sings and schooner races, Dixieland jazz cruises and band concerts, and demonstrations of everything from salting a fish to making a baggywrinkle. In the winter, when there's more time, visitors can try their hands at open-hearth cooking, quilting, scrimshanding (making scrimshaw), sewing sails, and net-making. And, if you're in Mystic at Christmastime, you will have the most special experience of your life.

Mystic Seaport is truly a wonderful and amazing place that should be seen by every American at least once in his lifetime.

Mystic Seaport is located on Route 27 about one-half mile south of Exit 90 of I-95. The hours in the summer season (April through November) are 9 a.m. to 5 p.m., and in the winter season (December through March) are 10 a.m. to 4 p.m. Admission during the summer season is $5.50 for adults and $2.75 for children (6 to 12); in the summer, a two-day ticket may be purchased for $7 for adults and $3.50 for children. Admission during the winter season is $4.50 for adults and $2.25 for children (again, 6 to 12). Special rates are available for older students and senior citizens.

Mystic Marinelife Aquarium — More than 600,000 visitors each year make this highly respected aquarium the most popular attraction in Connecticut. And that's understandable: this is one of the finest smaller oceanariums in the world. The wonderful thing about this organization is that they see their primary role as educational and secondarily as a form of entertainment. The displays are teaching displays, and the shows are centered more on describing why the animals do what they do and how they do it as opposed to degrading and humiliating them by making them perform silly antics. Not that there isn't any fun and laughter here, there's plenty of that. The point is that at this facility, the thrust is towards research and learning.

On the first level, there are 30 living exhibits containing more than 2000 specimens. These displays are broken into two major themes: Adaptation and Aquatic Communities. This use of major themes to tie together a series of exhibits is unique among oceanariums.

Each exhibit in the Adaptation section shows one technique that marine organisms have evolved to better survive in the sea. For example, the flounder and the sea raven, among others, display protective coloration techniques that render them almost invisible in their environment. Other fishes school, defend territories, utilize symbiosis in a dangerous environment, or use venom in defense. One display from which it is almost impossible to tear yourself away is the yellow-headed jawfish, a fascinating territorial defender, who, much like his human counterpart, relies on the big bluff to achieve his objectives. Other interesting displays in this section include flashlight fish from the Red Sea, anemone-fish, and a bunch of charming little sea horses.

The Aquatic Communities theme is divided into three geographical areas: New England Waters, The Tropical Atlantic, and The Pacific Coast.

The New England displays include a huge tank with some of the area's commercially valuable fishes: cod, pollack, flounder and scup. Also, there are displays of a wharf-piling community, a fresh water pond, and a salt marsh. The largest exhibit in the Tropical Atlantic section shows the inhabitants of tropical shallow reefs. Two green turtles swim among groups of brilliantly-colored fishes such as the queen trigger, the gray angel, and the French grunt; a large moray eel lurks in the coral outcroppings and the bottom is patrolled by spiny lobsters. In the Pacific Coast section, there are displays of anemones, California kelp fishes, and a giant 30-pound Pacific octopus.

The largest exhibit on the main level is a circular 30,000-gallon tank with 16 viewing windows called "The Open Sea." Here are some of the larger fish found in New England waters including bluefish, striped bass, and a variety of sharks.

The Marine Theater, a 1,400-seat auditorium designed especially for marine mammal demonstrations, is located on the second level. Beginning at 10 a.m. every day, the hourly demonstrations, held in the 350,000-gallon center pool, feature the only whales in New England. Alex, a one-ton belukha whale (whom you will love instantly because of his smiling face and peaceful disposition), and the smaller female, Okanitoo, star in a show that also includes a pair of bottlenose dolphins and some California sea lions. The shows are really training sessions with the public as observers. These demonstrations are entertaining *and* educational and are worth ten times the admission price to the aquarium.

Photo Courtesy of Mystic Marinelife Aquarium

Alex

Seal Island, just recently opened and occupying two and one-half acres adjacent to the aquarium, has been constructed so as to simulate the shoreline typical of the various seals' native environments. One of the pools contains New England harbor seals and several big gray seals. Another has a collection of northern fur seals, and a third has some playful California sea lions and three young elephant seals named Gurgle, Gronk, and Grumble. The interior of the island has information displays and excellent slide shows describing the habits and environment of seals. This has been a great addition to an already superior aquarium. A tank being constructed at the main entrance to the main building will house two huge Steller's sea lions.

The Mystic Marinelife Aquarium is located right at Exit 90 of I-95. It is open daily (except Thanksgiving, Christmas, and New Year's Day) from 9 a.m. to evening. Admission is $4.50 for adults and $2 for children (5 to 14). Admission to the aquarium includes the demonstrations and a visit to Seal Island. For a general information recording, call 203-536-3323.

Mystic Walking Tour — The waterfront area of downtown Mystic is literally packed with wonderful old homes, most of them built by men who made their living from the sea. The Mystic Junior Woman's Club and the Mystic Chamber of Commerce have put together a super walking tour of the section of town on the western shore of the Mystic River. The histories of the houses as well as the careers of their builders are described in detail. Also, anything of architectural interest is noted. Copies of the tour may be picked up at the Tourist Information Bureau or at the Chamber of Commerce (in the old railroad station on Route 1).

Whitehall Mansion — Whitehall Mansion was built in 1775 on what is believed to be the foundation of a much earlier house (c. 1690). In fact, there is much evidence that the kitchen fireplace is a relic of that earlier home. Maintained by the Stonington Historical Society, this fine country mansion has been beautifully restored and tastefully furnished with eighteenth-century objects. The kitchen fireplace has a rare "trimmer arch" that supports the hearthstone of the fireplace on the second floor. The windows, all "twelve-over-twelves," and the three-foot cedar shingles are special treats. The Historical Society keeps an extensive genealogical and historical library on the second floor which is open regularly and is available to researchers. The Stonington Garden Club maintains a wonderful colonial herb garden on the grounds.

The Whitehall Mansion is located off Route 27 just north

of Exit 90 of I-95. It is directly across the street from the Wine Cellar. The house is open from May 1 to October 31 from 2 p.m. to 4 p.m., daily except Saturday. Admission is 75¢ for adults and 25¢ for children.

Whitehall Burying Ground — The Whitehall Burying Ground is on a pretty hill overlooking the Mystic River and has a well-preserved and interesting collection of eighteenth-century headstones. Many of the early settlers of the area are buried here as well as a number of freed slaves. The cemetery is located across Route 27 from the Whitehall Mansion; turn down the path between the Cash Home Center and the Farm Maid store.

Denison Pequotsepos Nature Center — Like the Thames Science Center in New London, the Denison Pequotsepos Nature Center is maintained by a private, non-profit group dedicated to educating the community about ecology and the environment. The Trailside Museum is packed with exhibits of birds, eggs, fossils, and many other interesting natural history displays. In addition, there are live exhibits of snakes, turtles, and other reptiles. An excellent gift shop offers books, birdfeeders, and various items concerned with nature and the environment. This museum is very complete and special, and would be particularly fascinating for the youngsters.

The 125-acre wildlife sanctuary is laced with about four miles of self-guiding trails (a map of the area is available at the museum). There is even a nature trail for the blind, with descriptions posted in braille. Several large flying cages house a variety of owls and hawks. During the summer months, a guided tour of the sanctuary is given every Wednesday at 1:30 p.m. and is an event that should not be missed.

To get there, take the road that runs behind Olde Mistick Village and the aquarium and turn right on Jerry Browne Road. At the top of the hill, turn right on Pequotsepos Road and go about one-half mile. The Denison Pequotsepos Nature Center is across the street from the Denison Homestead, and is open in the summer Monday through Saturday from 9 a.m. to 5 p.m., and on Sunday from 1 p.m. to 5 p.m. In the winter, the hours are 10 a.m. to 4 p.m. Tuesday through Saturday, and 1 p.m. to 4 p.m. on Sunday. Admission is 75¢ for adults, 40¢ for children (under 6 free).

Photo Courtesy of Connecticut Development Commission

Denison Homestead, Colonial Kitchen

Denison Homestead — Originally built in 1717, this house was occupied by eleven successive generations of Denisons. In 1941, the last resident, Ann Borodell Denison Gates, bequeathed her home to a family association for use as a museum. This house is unique in the area. The Denisons apparently stored everything they ever owned or used over the 224 years they occupied the house, so when the homestead was restored, it was decided to show the progressive changes in Connecticut living over a two-century time span, and the result is fascinating.

The kitchen is colonial with the typical enormous fireplace and a nice collection of early utensils. The parlor is furnished in the Federal style and shows what living was like in the early 1800s. The living room was left as it was in 1941, so there are some familiar twentieth-century accoutrements. Upstairs, one of the bedrooms is furnished in the period of the Revolutionary War, while the other is done in the Civil War manner, reflecting life in the 1860s. The feeling of transition in seeing living styles and tastes change as you go from room to room is interesting and sometimes dramatic. This is an amazing home.

To reach the Denison Homestead, refer to the directions to the Denison Pequotsepos Nature Center which is across the street. The house is open from May 15 to October 15, daily except Monday, from 1 p.m. to 5 p.m. Admission is $1.25 for adults and 25¢ for youngsters 6 to 16.

Indian and Colonial Research Center — During her lifetime, Eva L. Butler, a historian and archaeologist, amassed an incredible collection of books and manuscripts concerning Indians and the early colonists. This collection is now housed in the Indian and Colonial Research Center and is available to researchers, genealogists, and the general public on a regular basis. The building itself is interesting: it was built in 1856 and served as the home of the Mystic National Bank for many years.

The center is located on Route 27 in the center of Old Mystic, about two miles north of Exit 90 of I-95. It is open year-round on Tuesdays, Thursdays, and Saturdays from 2 p.m. to 4 p.m.

Olde Mistick Village — While it is not the purpose of this guide to promote commercial establishments, a visit to Olde Mystick Village can be a treat for any visitor. Located at Exit 90 of I-95 next to the Mystic Marinelife Aquarium, this shopping center, built and laid out like an old town, is crammed with interesting and exciting small shops offering just about anything your heart may desire. The Tourist Information Bureau is located here, as well as the Memory Lane Doll Museum.

Memory Lane Doll Museum — What started off as a tiny hobby some 10 years ago has grown into one of the largest collections of dolls in America. Violet Meier, the curator, will take you on a tour of this astounding group of more than 1,000 dolls and describe their histories and uses. Dating from 1800 to the present day, the dolls come from almost every country in the world and are made of just about every conceivable material. There is a large collection of Shirley Temple dolls from the 1930s, including a big moving one that has Shirley playing an organ and singing. Mortimer Snerd, Batman, Jackie Robinson, Charlie McCarthy, and W. C. Fields can also be found here. Pay special attention to Buster Brown and his dog Tige (who actually barks). In addition to the dolls, there are many toys on display including old trains, cars, fire engines, and a Schoenut Circus. Even Dad will enjoy this entertaining and unusual museum.

The museum is found in Building 4 of Olde Mistick Village. It is open daily from 10 a.m. to 6 p.m., Sundays from noon to 6 p.m. Admission is 50¢ for adults and 25¢ for children 5 to 12.

Dining

★**Yesterday's Manner** — Although Yesterday's Manner was just recently opened, it is already recognized as one of the best restaurants in Connecticut. The setting for this fine establishment is a large century-old barn that has been completely renovated and subtly embellished, and the surprising result is quiet, old-fashioned elegance. The tables are spaced far apart on both the main floor and in the open loft, so if intimacy and privacy are part of your itinerary, this is the place to go. Even the soft piano music that accompanies the meal is unobtrusive and pleasant. The restaurant's motto is "the pace and grace of years past," and it's true. The pace may be slow and peaceful, but the service (provided by a group of enthusiastic young waiters) is the best we've encountered. This is a wonderful restaurant in every respect.

The menu features about twenty French and Continental dishes, all of them excellent. The preparation is superb: the sauces and condiments enhance the food rather than hide it, and the whole thing shows that the kitchen really cares. Among the various duckling, veal, beef, and seafood selections, we would hesitate to pick and choose, but the roast duckling with olive sauce, the veal marsala, and the bouillabaisse are unsurpassed. Prices for the entrees range from $7.95 to $10.95, but if this restaurant were in New York, the prices would be double, and there would be lines around the block waiting to get in. The wine list features something for everyone at a fair price. A varied dessert menu features several exotic items, but if you have no regard for your waistline, order their incredible chocolate mousse. You will not be disappointed with Yesterday's Manner — this is one of the finest restaurants around and is worth a long drive.

Yesterday's Manner is located on Route 184 in Old Mystic. Take Route 27 north from Exit 90 of I-95 and go through the village to Route 184; turn right and in about one-half mile, the restaurant will appear on your left. Only dinner is served and the restaurant is closed on Mondays. The hours are 4:30 p.m. to 9:30 p.m. on Tuesday through Thursday, 4:30 p.m. to 10:30 p.m. on Friday and Saturday, and 4:30 p.m. to 9 p.m. on Sunday. Reservations are recommended. Credit cards: AE, BA/V, DC, MC. 203-536-1228.

The Mischievous Carrot — Don't let the fact that this is a natural foods restaurant turn you off, for at the Mischievous Carrot you will get a fine meal for an astoundingly low price. Sure, if you're into sprouts or yogurt with raisins, there's plenty of that. But there's a lot else too, including a friendly and relaxed atmosphere with chamber music and small wooden tables. The kitchen is actually a part of the dining room, protected only by a macrame screen, so the smells and the quiet activity are very much a part of your meal.

The salads and sandwiches are a delight! The "Raw Vegie Salad Plate" is not only excellent, but is the most expensive item on the menu at $2.50. Among the sandwiches we've enjoyed are the curried egg salad ($1.60) and the tostada ($1.75). The soup of the day is always good no matter what it is, and don't pass up the rich and tasty smoothies ($1). They are especially proud of their sweets, which are served from a buffet; the carrot cake is wonderful. The hot specials, featuring everything from fresh fish to fettucini, change every month, with one or two offered each day.

The Mischievous Carrot is found on Holmes Street in downtown Mystic, just before the drawbridge: look for a sign that has a carrot on it. Lunch is served from 11 a.m. to 2 p.m. Monday through Friday and from 11:30 a.m. to 3 p.m. on Saturday and Sunday. Dinner hours are 6 p.m. to 9 p.m. daily. Tea is served each afternoon between lunch and dinner, and a brunch is available on Sunday. No reservations, no credit cards, no smoking. 203-536-7126.

Seamen's Inn — Located on Route 27 at the northern edge of the Mystic Seaport complex, the Seamen's Inn carries on the Seaport environment with tasteful nautical decor. Ship models, figureheads, and paintings abound and give one the feeling that this is just one more exhibit. Obviously designed to handle large crowds in the spacious dining rooms, the hustle and bustle is not an obvious part of your meal, and, if the turnover is high, you are generally not aware of it.

Visitors to the Seaport are looking for a bit of old New England, and this restaurant carries on that desire with a menu of traditional New England dishes. Besides the usual steaks and chops, duckling, chicken, and a wide selection of seafood are available. The average price of an entree runs about $9 and includes a salad and a choice of potato or vegetable; the servings are generous. The Boston Scrod ($8.50) is particularly good as is the Seafood Crepes ($7.95) and the Scallops Polanaise ($8.50). The prime ribs and steaks are above average, not only in quality, but in preparation. Luncheons include a full range of sandwiches, salads, and entrees at prices of $3.25 to $4.95.

The Seamen's Inn is on Route 27 next to the north entrance to Mystic Seaport. It is open seven days a week from 11:30 a.m. to 9 p.m. They do not accept reservations. Credit cards: AE, BA/V, DC, MC. 203-536-9649.

Chuck's Steak House — Here is one of the places that the hungry meat-eater should head. Chuck's, a chain known coast to coast, is renowned for its uncomplicated decor and its excellent food. Occupying one wing of an old tool and die factory, the setting here is above average and interesting. A pleasant, relaxed solarium-lounge upstairs provides good views of Mystic harbor, and there's always a fire going in a large, free-standing fireplace.

The menu consists of about a dozen beef and seafood dishes, all of them very good. Prices range from $5.95 (beef kabob) to $9.95 (lobster tails). The best thing about Chuck's is the size of the helpings in relation to the price. For example, the New York strip steak ($7.95) weighs in at 12 oz. and the prime rib ($8.75) is 16 oz. to 20 oz. Dinner prices include bread and salad; baked potatoes are an additional 65¢. If you want a good meal, cooked to a turn, at a fair price, it's hard to beat Chuck's.

Chuck's Steak House is located at 12 Water Street just west of downtown Mystic. Take the road towards Noank and the restaurant will be on your right at the top of the hill. They do not accept reservations, so expect a wait on summer weekends. Chuck's is open for dinner only, daily from 5 p.m. to 10 p.m. Credit cards: AE, BA/V, MC. 203-536-4589.

Mystic

Steak Loft — The Steak Loft is a refreshing change from the nautical fish houses: the theme here is barnyard instead of shipyard. The walls are rough-sawn pine, and the lounge has a loft filled with old wagons, sleighs, and farm implements. The lounge is enormous but it has charm and warmth; you can even carve your initials in the bar, so bring a knife. Piano players or small bands provide weekend entertainment. Plans are on the drawing board to add an outdoor clam bar adjacent to the lounge.

Several nice dining rooms are available to handle the crowds. Dinner entrees consist of a limited selection of steaks, chicken, and seafood. The combinations of steak with various things are very good (try the steak and shrimp: excellent). The prices of these combinations range from $7.95 to $11.95, while the steaks go for $6.50 to $10.95. But those who are hungry and looking for a big piece of meat may be disappointed here; for example, the "Heavy Cut" of New York sirloin, costing $10.95, is only 12 oz. All entrees include a trip to a great salad bar and a choice of baked potato or steak fries. Children have their own menu with the usual stuff at reasonable prices. At lunch, you have a choice of eating in the dining room or the lounge. The menu is basically the same except that the dining room prices are about $1 more (but that includes french fries and salad bar). Prices are generally in the $2 to $4 range.

If you are looking for good honest food and drink, the Steak Loft won't let you down, but, because they don't accept reservations, the wait can be an hour or more during the summer.

The Steak Loft is located in Olde Mistick Village, right at Exit 90 of I-95. They are open for lunch daily from 11:30 a.m. to 2:30 p.m. Dinner is served from 4:30 p.m. to 9:30 p.m. Monday through Thursday, 4:30 p.m. to 10:30 p.m. Friday and Saturday, and 4:30 p.m. to 9 p.m. on Sunday. Credit cards: AE, BA/V, CB, DC, MC. 203-536-2661.

Groton

(Including Burnett's Corner, Center Groton, Groton Long Point, Noank, and Poquonock Bridge)

Calling itself the "Submarine Capital of the World" is not an idle boast on Groton's part, for located here is the largest sub base in the Western Hemisphere as well as the Electric Boat Division of General Dynamics, the largest private manufacturer of submarines in the world. A nuclear submarine cruising up the river, an event that would turn out the whole county anywhere else, is a common occurrence in Groton and is almost ignored.

Originally a part of New London, Groton incorporated as a separate town in 1705. Surrounded on three sides by water—the Thames River, Long Island Sound, and the Mystic River—Groton naturally turned its attention to the sea. The town shared with New London a long history of whaling, shipping, and privateering. Unfortunately, it also shared a sad part in the British raid of Sept. 6, 1781.

While part of the British invasion force concentrated on New London and Fort Trumbull, another 800 seasoned regulars landed in Groton to attack Fort Griswold. The fort was still under construction and was manned by about 150 inexperienced and hastily assembled militiamen, so the position was soon overwhelmed. The American commander, Col. William Ledyard, seeing that the battle was lost, ordered his men to throw down their arms and surrender. As was the custom, he offered his sword to the British commander, who immediately ran Ledyard through with it. The British troops then ran amuck and killed and mutilated most of the men remaining in the fort. In all, more than 80 Americans died at Fort Griswold in what was one of the bloodiest massacres of the Revolutionary War. But for the inside information provided by the traitor, Benedict Arnold, it might not have been such a disaster. Upon sighting the British fleet in the river, two cannon shots (the sound of alarm) were fired from the fort. Immediately after the second shot, a third shot (the signal of good news) was fired from one of the British frigates, thereby keeping the citizens of Groton from gathering and organizing an adequate defense.

The section of Mystic west of the Mystic River is a part of Groton, but, for purposes of this guide, Mystic has been treated as a separate town.

Things to see & do

Groton is a heavily industrialized town with the consequent warehouses, factories, and collections of small homes and apartments. The community of Noank, however, is worth a trip. Formerly a small fishing and shipbuilding village, the town today is a charming, quiet summer colony where most of the homes have wonderful views. A walk up Riverview Avenue provides a commanding vista of the entrance to Mystic harbor and Mason's Island. From the foot of Pearl Street, one can get a good view of the boat basin to the west and the beginning of Fishers Island Sound.

Fort Griswold State Park and Groton Monument — Fort Griswold, site of the bloody battle in September, 1781, is today a peaceful group of meadows on a hill overlooking New London and the Thames River. The outlines of the original fort can still be discerned and some of the fortifications are intact, so it does not take too much imagination to picture the British troops storming the walls and terrorizing the town. (If imagination isn't enough for you, the battle is reenacted every Labor Day weekend.) Battle or not, this is a beautiful place to wander around.

Across the street is the Groton Battle Monument, a granite obelisk dedicated in 1830 and erected in honor of the brave men who defended the fort. From the top, 134 feet up, one has a fabulous view of the Sound, the offshore islands, and the Thames River valley. Next to the Monument is Monument House, a museum with relics of the battle, Indian costumes and artifacts, and some whaling memorabilia.

The park is on Monument Avenue up the hill south of the *Croaker* Memorial; the obelisk can be seen from everywhere, so just head towards it. The Monument and Monument House are open daily from Memorial Day to October 12, from 8:30 a.m. to 4 p.m., Sundays from 9 a.m. to 5 p.m. Admission is free. The park is open daily year-round from sunrise to sunset.

Photo Courtesy of Connecticut Department of Commerce

Groton Battle Monument and Monument House

29

Ebenezer Avery House — After the violence at Fort Griswold had subsided, British officers, finally showing some mercy, decided to take American wounded down the hill to the river to get them help. The dying and wounded men were loaded into an ammunition wagon which, gathering momentum, soon went out of control and shot down the hillside, striking a stump directly in front of the Ebenezer Avery house, then located near the shore. The men, including Avery himself, were thrown about, and several were killed. The remaining wounded were brought into the house by British soldiers, but medical help was not forthcoming until the next morning; during the night more of the men died. The bloodstains from this event were evident on the floors of the house for many years. Built about 1750 by Ensign Ebenezer Avery, this ten-room house has been faithfully restored and is a good example of the center-chimney colonial style popular in the mid-1700s. Most of the furnishings in the house are from the latter part of the eighteenth century, and almost all of them were contributed by Avery descendants. Of particular interest is an indoor smokehouse and the signatures on panes of glass of two of Avery's four wives (all of whom, curiously, were named Elizabeth).

The house is located on the grounds of Fort Griswold State Park, directly down the hill from the main entrance. It is open from 2 p.m. to 4 p.m. on Friday, Saturday, and Sunday during June, July, and August. Admission is free.

Submarine Memorial — The *U.S.S. Croaker* — Launched in Groton in 1944, the *Croaker* is a veteran of six patrols in the Pacific during World War II. Here is a first-class chance to come aboard and explore a real submarine, from torpedo rooms to galleys. Tours are conducted by ex-submariners who are more than willing to answer any questions. This is a fascinating experience. From the site of the *Croaker,* there's a good view of the General Dynamics shipyard, which is currently building the enormous Trident class of nuclear-powered submarine. The Memorial is engaged in a project whereby the first and most famous nuclear sub, the *Nautilus,* will be returned to Groton and opened to the public.

To reach the *Croaker* from I-95 eastbound, take the Bridge Street exit and follow the signs to Thames Street; westbound, take the Gales Ferry exit and follow the signs. The *Croaker* is open from 9 a.m. to 5 p.m. daily from April 15 to October 15, and from 9 a.m. to 3:30 p.m. daily from October 16 to April 14. Admission is $2 for adults and $1 for children under 12.

Photo By John Urwiller

New London and the *U.S.S. Croaker*

"See the Submarines By Boat" Tour — This is a one-hour, seven-mile cruise on the Thames River. Besides getting a close look at the largest submarine base in the Western Hemisphere, the cruise will take you past the Coast Guard Academy, the General Dynamics shipyard, and the Naval Underwater Systems Center. A narration during the tour describes all the sights, and relates the history of this famous river. This cruise is excellent for young and old alike.

To get there, take Bridge Street to Fairview Avenue and turn north under the Gold Star Bridge. Tours are held daily from May 20 to September 10 between 9 a.m. and 4:30 p.m. Admission is $3 for adults and $1.25 for children 4 to 12.

31

Gray Line Bus Tours — The Gray Line offers several tours of the New London-Groton area, and they are all fun. The bus tour of the Naval Submarine Base is the only way to get into the place, and you are able to ride within a few feet of our latest nuclear subs and their floating drydocks. A special treat on this tour is a visit to the Submarine Forces Museum, which is filled with historical information and memorabilia. The story about the toilet paper in World War II is worth the entire fare. This particular tour includes a visit to the *U.S.S. Croaker.* Most of the Gray Line tours are run seasonally or irregularly, so call ahead for information. On weekdays, call 203-443-1831; on weekends, call 203-447-1727.

Noank Museum — Maintained by the Noank Historical Society, the Noank Museum devotes itself to preserving and displaying items from the early history of the town. Because Noank was occupied by Indians until 1742, there is a large display of Indian artifacts. Shipbuilding was a major industry for many years, and a great deal of the museum's collection concerns itself with this activity. Displays include photographs, relics, models, and documents; their collection of early shipbuilding tools is particularly outstanding. One interesting display shows photographs of the *Dauntless* breaking up off the coast of Africa. It seems that the captain had gone ashore to take pictures of his ship when a sudden squall drove her up on the rocks. This is the finest small museum we've encountered. If you're in Noank, you should spend some time seeing it. And if you wish to walk through this charming village, you can pick up a walking guide to historic Noank here.

The museum can be found in an old stone church on Sylvan Street in Noank. It is open from July 4 to Labor Day, from 2 p.m. to 5 p.m. The rest of the year, the museum is open on Wednesdays from 2 p.m. to 5 p.m. Admission is a 25¢ donation.

Bluff Point Coastal Reserve — Bluff Point is the largest undeveloped coastal tract between New York and Cape Cod, and is a paradise for hikers and bird-watchers. Motor vehicles are not permitted inside this 800-acre park; all exploring must be done on foot. From the tip of the rocky promontory that juts into the Sound, a wonderful view of Fishers Island and the Sound can be enjoyed. This spot is about a mile and a half from the parking area and can be reached on any of several different trails. Be sure to take your bathing suit because there is a mile-long unspoiled beach extending from the southern tip of the peninsula. When returning to the car, take the trail east towards Mumford Cove. The round trip is about four miles, every bit of it beautiful and peaceful. The parking area is located at the end of Depot Road (off Route 1 just west of the Town Hall in Center Groton).

Esker Point — Esker Point is a fine little public park located on Groton Long Point Road just west of Noank and across the street from the Yankee Fisherman restaurant. The beach is fairly small but very pleasant, and a shady grove protects a well-equipped picnic ground. Parking is across the street adjacent to the restaurant.

Dining

Abbott's Lobster in the Rough — Anyone visiting New England has to have at least one lobster and steamer orgy, and Abbott's is about as good a place as any to let it all hang out. This is a style of restaurant very popular along the Maine coast: a place where you can sit outdoors at gaily painted picnic tables (or indoors if it's raining), enjoy a fine view, and be as messy as you want to be. Vistas of Long Island Sound and Fishers Island accompany your meal and, if the kids get a little antsy, they can climb around on the rocks and ledges that line the shore.

Just place your order at the counter, get a number and wait until it's called (usually about 30 minutes). The main attraction, of course, is lobster, available in several different sizes. Prices vary according to the catch, but you will have a hard time beating Abbott's price. In addition, various soups, steamers, stuffed fried clams, and lobster, crab, and shrimp rolls are available. Melted butter, coleslaw, and potato chips come with each meal.

This is a wonderful, informal, no-frills place where the food is terrific and the price is fair. Be sure to bring your own beverage. A retail shop is adjacent to the restaurant so you can take home everything from lobster to lobster bisque. A dock is available for the hungry yachtsman.

Abbott's is located near the foot of Pearl Street in Noank village. It is open from May 1 to Labor Day daily from 11 a.m. to 9 p.m. Abbott's does not accept credit cards.

Yankee Fisherman — Overlooking Palmer Cove, this restaurant is very much oriented to the water and if you're lucky, you can get a window table with a great view. As you drive up, a rowboat on davits, portholes, fishnets, and anchors welcome you to this establishment and give you the idea that seafood might be available. The interior decoration is also nautical, with crowds of pictures, navigation instruments, ship models, and other relics of sailing vessels, all of it authentic and pleasant. The tables are widely spaced and each has a brass candleholder and comfortable captain's chairs. The lounge is cozy with a fireplace crackling on cold days and nights.

The menu states that all produce, fish, and pies are fresh daily, and the quality of the food generally reflects this concern and care. Yankee Fisherman features seafood but has several selections of steak and duck. The specialty of the house is the Capt's Bowl of Sea Food Stew (bouillabaisse) which is huge and delicious. This is one of the few fish houses we have experienced where the deep-fried fish is light and does not seem as if it had spent the better part of the day at the bottom of some broiling pot. Try the cabbage salad: a treat. Dinners range from $5.00 to $9.50. Luncheon has an assortment of fish dishes plus sandwiches with prices ranging from $2.50 to $4.75. The Yankee Fisherman is a real "salty" restaurant but, this time, has the food to match the decor.

This restaurant is located on Groton Long Point Road just west of Noank Village and across from Esker Point on the Sound. It is open from 11:30 a.m. to 3 p.m. and 5 p.m. to 10 p.m. on Tuesday through Saturday, and from noon to 9 p.m. on Sunday (when a Sunday brunch is offered). Yankee Fisherman is closed on Monday. Reservations are suggested, especially during the summer. Credit cards: AE, BA/V, DC, MC. 203-536-1717 or 203-535-0101.

New London

Founded in 1646 by John Winthrop, Jr., New London was once much larger, encompassing the present towns of Groton and Waterford. In the earliest days, this town was a part of the Massachusetts Bay Colony; it was settled because of its excellent deep-water harbor, one of the best on the East Coast. Because of this harbor, the town's orientation has always been towards the sea.

While Nantucket and New Bedford come to mind first as famous whaling ports, New London was one of the biggest and busiest in the world: for more than a century, as many as 80 ships based here roamed the oceans of the world in search of whales, and several vast fortunes were accumulated. Evidence of some of this wealth can be seen in Whale Oil Row on Huntington Street, where there are four incredible 1830 Greek Revival homes in a row, the only such group in the United States. When oil was discovered in Pennsylvania in 1859, the whaling industry went into a sharp decline, and manufacturing became the dominant industry. In the latter part of the nineteenth century, the character of the city began to change when large numbers of immigrants arrived to fill the labor pool. Today, New London is embarked on an ambitious downtown renovation project which, we hope, will return the city to its former charm.

New London figured prominently in both the Revolutionary War and the War of 1812. During the Revolution, so many privateers used New London harbor as a base that the British were forced to take drastic action. On Sept. 6, 1781, more than 800 troops under the command of turncoat Benedict Arnold

35

landed and overwhelmed Fort Trumbull (now the site of the U.S. Navy Underwater Systems Center). The British then started to burn ships and supplies, and when the wind shifted, almost the entire center of New London went up in flames. It was during this battle that one of the worst massacres of the war took place across the river (see Groton). During the War of 1812, the British blockaded New London for almost two years, keeping Commodore Decatur's fleet bottled up in the river. When news of the end of the war reached New London on Feb. 21, 1815, the British landed and graciously presented the town with the Peace Bell.

Things to see & do

Because there are so many interesting things to do in New London, they are presented here in geographical order, beginning in the northern part of the city and working towards the coast.

Connecticut Arboretum — One of the finest arboretums in the state is found on Williams Street across from the Connecticut College campus. The arboretum, now comprising approximately 415 acres, maintains an extensive collection of native trees and shrubs, wildflower preserves, several demonstration areas in vegetation management, and two natural tracts for ecological research. About 375 species of woody plants indigenous to the Northeast can be identified here. The land is laced with paths, and there are flowers and lovely groves everywhere. Several picnic areas have been set aside for those who choose to spend some time in this quiet and beautiful place. A map of the arboretum and some informative pamphlets describing the various trees and plants to be seen there can be picked up at the Connecticut College Information Office or at the Thames Science Center. Enter the campus from Route 32 about one mile north of I-95 and drive directly across to Williams Street. The arboretum is open daily from sunrise to sunset. There is no admission charge.

Thames Science Center — Established in 1952, the Thames Science Center serves the community as an educational instrument to expand knowledge about the environment and ecological conservation. A fine museum room is especially appealing to children: it has live-animal exhibits, saltwater aquariums, and displays of shells, minerals, and fossils. Anything and everything can be handled, but watch out for the tarantula. Another room has a working solar hot water system on exhibit. A small but complete book and gift shop oriented to nature and the environment is found in the lobby. If you need an identification book or a birdfeeder, buy it here; they can use the money and they're doing some wonderful things. The Science Center is on the grounds of the Connecticut Arboretum on Gallows Lane just off Williams Street. It is open year-round from 9 a.m. to 4 p.m. Monday through Saturday, and from 1 p.m. to 5 p.m. on Sunday. Admission is free.

Photo By John Urwiller

Lyman Allyn Museum, South Entrance

Lyman Allyn Museum — Housed in an impressive building, the Lyman Allyn Museum covers more than 5000 years of man's history. On permanent display are galleries of Egyptian, Greek, and Roman Antiquities; Medieval and Renaissance Art; Oriental and Primitive Art; and American and European paintings, furniture, silver, and decorative arts. In addition, four galleries are devoted to changing exhibitions throughout the year. All the exhibits are beautifully displayed and described, and the visitor has a hard time remembering that all this is in New London and not New York or Washington. The lower level has an absolutely incredible collection of doll houses and furniture. For scholars and researchers, a vast collection of art history books is available on a non-circulating basis in the Museum Library. Also, the museum has an excellent restoration laboratory. This is a super museum and should not be missed.

The main entrance is off Williams Street just south of the Connecticut College campus. The museum is open Tuesday through Saturday from 1 p.m. to 5 p.m., and on Sunday from 2 p.m. to 5 p.m. Admission is free, but donations are appreciated.

Deshon-Allyn House — Built in 1829, this large granite house is now a part of the Lyman Allyn Museum. Only three rooms are open to the public (the rest of the house serves as the home of the Director), but if you are interested in the formal elegance of the mid-nineteenth century, you should see this place. Completely restored in 1956, the furnishings are in the late Federal and Empire styles and accurately reflect the manner in which a wealthy whaling merchant lived during the mid-1800s. Of particular interest are a nine-foot secretary, an American Empire sofa and chairs, and many paintings and portraits.

The house is opened only on request: see a guard at the Lyman Allyn Museum during regular museum hours. Admission is free.

United States Coast Guard Academy — The Coast Guard Academy is open daily from 9 a.m. to sunset and offers the visitor a close-up look at a military academy at work. The first stop should be at the new Visitors' Pavilion, where there are some nice displays and a 20-minute slide presentation about the Coast Guard. A brochure available at the pavilion describes an excellent walking tour of the beautiful grounds. If you're lucky, you might see a full-dress parade. When the 295-foot training bark *Eagle,* the pride of America's Tall Ships, is at her mooring (usually from September through June), visitors are welcomed aboard after working hours or on weekends. There is no admission charge for any of this. The Academy is a very special place to take youngsters. The main entrance is on Route 32 about three-quarters of a mile north of I-95.

Ye Ancientist Burial Ground — Located at 190 Huntington Street near I-95, this is the oldest cemetery in New London County, with the first recorded burial taking place in 1653. Almost every headstone is well preserved and most of them date from before the Revolution. The cemetery is found on a hill with a good view of the town and the river, and it is said that from this spot Benedict Arnold watched the British troops burning New London in September of 1781.

Ye Old Town Mill — Nowhere in the area does the past and present of New England come into closer juxtaposition than at this spot. Nestled against a small brook and surrounded by trees, this mill, originally built by John Winthrop, Jr., in 1650, is directly beneath the twin spans of the ultra-modern ten-lane Gold Star Bridge. Fully restored in 1960, the mill now has the working machinery and accoutrements of a typical nineteenth-century grain mill. The waterwheel is temporarily out of action, but this ancient building, which has many of the original beams in place, is well worth a stop. Photographers will have a field day.

Located at 8 Mill Street, the grounds are open year-round. The building itself is open from June 1 to Sept. 15 daily from 1 p.m. to 4 p.m. Admission is free.

Tale of the Whale Museum — It seems a shame that a town with a rich history in whaling does not support a museum dedicated to this early industry, but, luckily, in New London's case, a private citizen has shouldered the responsibility. Dr. Carl H. Wies, a wonderful old gent whose hobby has always been the whaling history of New London has, with his wife, put together a nifty collection of items concerned with whales and whaling. Dominated by a huge whaleboat from the *Charles Morgan* and the jawbone of a whale, the collection includes photographs and documents, harpoons, and ivory, scrimshaw and baleen items. Large charts trace the rise and fall of the whaling industry in the area. For the small fry, there is an excellent saltwater aquarium with horseshoe crabs, eels, and other charming and exotic creatures of the sea. A highlight of the museum is a 15-minute slide presentation narrated by the good doctor that describes the history and techniques of whaling. This is a fine small museum that should be included in your visit to New London.

Located at 3 Whale Oil Row (one of the four Greek Revival homes on Huntington Street), the museum is open every day except Monday from 1 p.m. to 5 p.m. Admission is 50¢ for adults and 35¢ for youngsters 6 to 16.

New London County Courthouse — Located on Huntington Street at the top of Captain's Walk, the New London County Courthouse was built in 1784 and has served as a courthouse for almost 200 years. It was here that the Peace Bell was presented to the town at the conclusion of the War of 1812. There's not much to see on the inside, but the building itself is handsome and interesting.

Nathan Hale Schoolhouse — Nathan Hale must have been a very restless man in his youth as there are a number of "Nathan Hale Schoolhouses" scattered around the state. It was from this particular one, however, that Hale left the teaching profession and entered the patriotic army, an event that eventually led to his being hanged as a spy by the British and his famous last words. This building was erected in 1774 and Hale taught here from March of that year until July of 1775. The schoolhouse is set up in the traditional bench style of those days.

Located in the mall area of Captain's Walk in downtown New London, the school is open daily during the summer months. There is no admission charge.

Shaw Mansion — This imposing stone structure was built in 1756 for Capt. Nathaniel Shaw by a group of Acadian refugees from Nova Scotia. Constructed entirely out of granite found on the property, this mansion is not at all typical of the usual mid-1700s home, but the stone construction is probably what saved it from destruction by fire during the battle of 1781. Shaw was a successful shipping merchant, and this gracious 21-room mansion well fitted his wealth and position. During the Revolution, this place served as the Naval Office for Connecticut, and the first naval expedition under Congress in 1776 was fitted out here. Among the notable persons to have stayed at this house are George Washington, Gen. Nathaniel Greene, Nathan Hale, and Gen. Lafayette. The house was occupied by Shaw descendants until 1907, when the New London County Historical Society purchased the property.

The rooms are large and sunny and are filled with treasures ranging from Benedict Arnold's sword and Napoleon's cup to wonderful collections of silver taken as booty during the privateering years. Pay attention to the walls: this is the only early house in the United States to have cement paneling. The collections of pewter, china, and oil portraits are also of special interest. The mansion houses an enormous collection of books and documents which are available to researchers. The grounds are lovely with a 1780 gazebo dominating the scene.

The Shaw Mansion is located at 11 Blinman Street, south of the center of town. It is open year-round, daily except Sunday and Monday from 1 p.m. to 4 p.m. Admission is 50¢ for adults and 25¢ for children.

Hempsted House — They should call this place Smithsonian North. Built in 1678 by Joshua Hempsted, this house was occupied continuously by Hempsted descendants until 1937. Today, it is maintained by the Antiquarian and Landmarks Society of Connecticut and is a *must* stop on any tour of the area. Having survived Benedict Arnold's burning of New London in 1781, it is the oldest house in New London and one of the oldest in Connecticut. Its restoration to the original seventeenth-century state has been incredible and any visitor is thrust back 300 years in time. From the giant oak summer beams and stone fireplaces to the casement windows and oak flooring, the house is exactly as it was three centuries ago.

The furnishings are all from the seventeenth and early eighteenth centuries and most of them outshine anything most

Photo Courtesy of Antiquarian and Landmarks Society

Hempsted House

museums can offer. There are treasures everywhere. Keep a lookout for a rare Windsor writing-arm chair, a British lantern clock, a child's walker built in 1742, and one of the finest collections of pewter anywhere. This is an exceptional house which will be enjoyed by the whole family. Mrs. Spitzer, the curator, is also exceptional, and will give you one of the best tours you'll ever have.

The house is located at the corner of Hempstead Street and Jay Street (Route 1A) near the downtown area of New London; there are plenty of signs. It is open from May 15 to October 15, daily except Monday, from 1 p.m. to 5 p.m. Admission is 75¢ for adults and 25¢ for youngsters under 16.

Huguenot House — Located on the grounds of the Hempsted House, this stone building, built during the 1750s, is undergoing an extensive restoration and should be open to the public sometime during the summer of 1980.

New London Ledge Lighthouse — When you're down at the point, you'll see what looks like a strange house sitting on a rock about a mile offshore. That's the New London Ledge Lighthouse. If you can get out there somehow, the keepers of this last manned lighthouse in Connecticut will welcome you between 10 a.m. and 4 p.m. daily, show you around and tell you all about Ernie the ghost.

Ocean Beach Park — Built in the late 1930s, Ocean Beach Park is in many ways an excellent example of a bygone era in beach entertainment. A long boardwalk follows the wide, curving beach and can provide the non-swimmer with a pleasant outing in the sun. There is an enormous swimming pool for those who eschew the beach experience, even though this is one of the nicest beaches around. The buildings are mostly done in the Art Deco and Bauhaus styles and are interesting architecturally. There are concessions of every variety, and a lot of the summer activity takes place around the amusement arcades and entertainment features. There's plenty of action and excitement here, but most people over 30 will probably find the park a bit too much.

There are varying parking and general admission fees depending on the time of day and the day of the week. The park is located at the foot of Ocean Avenue, about three miles from downtown New London near the O'Neill Theater Center.

Dining

★Ye Olde Tavern — In a business known for its high turnover, it's almost unheard of to see a restaurant under the same ownership for any length of time. Yet, Ye Olde Tavern has been owned by the same family since it was established in 1918. And judging from the testimonials, autographs, and photographs plastered all over the walls, everyone who has ever eaten here has had something good to say about it. So do we: this is a fine small restaurant serving the best meat around.

As soon as you are seated, hot garlic bread, a plate of delicious meatballs, a hunk of cheese, and a relish tray are spread before you. Enormous drinks arrive next, and you're ready to order. A sign on the outside says "House of Beef," and while that's what we would recommend, their lamb chops are excellent and their seafood specialties (served seasonally only) are superb. But back to the beef. The best deal in the house is a 30-oz. sirloin steak for two at $17.50. If you don't want to share, there's a 12-oz. sirloin for $7.50 or a 16-oz. New York cut for $9.75. On Saturday nights, you can have a 28-oz. prime rib for less than $11. A salad and potato are included with all entrees. The quality of the meat is outstanding, and they know how to cook it to perfection. There is a broad selection of appetizers and desserts at surprisingly fair prices. Ye Olde Tavern is quaint and pleasant and you will enjoy it. The only thing that bothered us (and not very much) is that the tables are fairly close and it has a tendency to become a little noisy.

Ye Olde Tavern is located at 345 Bank Street, about one-half mile south of the railroad station and adjacent to the Shaw Mansion. Serving dinner only, it is open from 5 p.m. to 10 p.m. Monday through Saturday, closed Sundays. Reservations are a must. Credit cards: AE, BA/V, CB, DC, MC. 203-442-0353.

Chuck's Steak House — Here's another Chuck's, this time one with a terrific view of the Thames River and Groton. As we have said before, if you want a good meal perfectly cooked at a fair price, head for Chuck's; you won't be disappointed.

The menu features about a dozen beef and seafood dishes plus some combinations at prices ranging from $5.95 to $9.95. The helpings are big and the food is great. (For further details, refer to Chuck's in Mystic.)

The restaurant is found at 250 Pequot Avenue about two miles south of downtown New London. Take Bank Street south from the railroad station and turn left on Howard Street which runs into Pequot Avenue. Chuck's is right next door to Burr's Marina. They do not accept reservations, so be prepared for a wait in a nice lounge on summer weekends. Dinner only, served between 5 p.m. and 10 p.m. daily. Credit cards: AE, BA/V, MC. 203-443-1323.

Romeo's — What do you do when you have an abandoned brick church on a busy highway? You turn it into a restaurant, of course. Romeo's has not only occupied the church, but has added a huge greenhouse to serve as the lounge. This is an attractive and busy establishment that also features some fine entertainment on weekends. Charcoal-broiled steaks and a good assortment of seafood dishes highlight a fairly broad dinner menu that also includes a few Italian dishes (which, incidentally, are very good). Prices range from $4.25 for spaghetti to $10.50 for the filet mignon with the average dinner going for about $7.50, including as many trips to the salad bar as you wish. The wine list is narrow, but good. The steaks are the most popular items on the menu with good reason; they're a decent size and always cooked to perfection.

A luncheon consisting of various kinds of hot and cold sandwiches can be enjoyed either in the dining room or in the Greenhouse lounge. Prices range from $2 to $3.50 in the dining room, but that, again, includes the salad bar. It's less expensive in the lounge, but no salad.

The dining room is open from 11 a.m. to 9 p.m. Monday through Friday; 4:30 p.m. to 9 p.m. on Saturday and Sunday. The lounge is open 11:30 a.m. to 1 a.m. Monday through Friday; 4:30 p.m. to 2 a.m. on Saturday, and 4:30 p.m. to 11 p.m. on Sunday. Reservations are recommended (especially on Saturday night). Credit cards: AE, BA/V, CB, MC. If traveling east on I-95, take Exit 83, and if going west, use Exit 84E. The restaurant is on Huntington Street just off I-95—you can see the sign from the road. 203-442-0439.

Waterford

(Including Pleasure Beach and Quaker Hill)

Originally a part of New London, Waterford (which incorporated as a separate town in 1801) has always, it seems, been fighting to protect its borders. In 1839, when East Lyme was created, Waterford lost a sizeable piece of its western lands to the new town. Next, in the 1890s, New London tried to annex the entire town and, after a prolonged fight in the General Assembly, New London was granted about two square miles of Waterford's territory. Finally, in 1911, New London again tried to annex the town; this time the attempt ended in failure. It is understandable that the more heavily populated town would be interested in Waterford as the latter has six times the land and about one-half the population of New London.

Waterford was first settled in the late seventeenth century with fishing and agriculture serving as the primary industries. Down the years, farming became the major source of livelihood, although there was some shipbuilding and quarrying activity; and in the mid-1800s several paper mills were located here. Today, Waterford is primarily a residential town serving Groton and New London. The town's shoreline is very pretty and hosts many summer visitors, although part of the shore is dominated by a huge nuclear power plant.

Things to see & do

Harkness Memorial State Park — If you've ever wondered how the other half lives, a visit to Harkness Memorial State Park is in order. Edward S. Harkness, an heir to a substantial fortune that came mostly from early investments in the Standard Oil Company, began construction of this summer mansion in 1904. The estate was added to and improved upon for decades. In the same philanthropic spirit that saw Harkness donate more than $200 million to various charities, his wife, upon her death in 1950, bequeathed the entire estate to the people of Connecticut to be used in a manner beneficial to public health. Today, fully half of the grounds and facilities are reserved as an exclusive recreation site for the state's handicapped.

The 234-acre estate is situated on a rocky promontory jutting into Long Island Sound near the confluence of the Thames River and the Sound, and is as beautiful as anything Newport has to offer. Besides the mansion itself, there are several spectacular outbuildings: one of them used to be the servants' quarters, and also housed garages, a stable, a bowling alley, a billiard room, and a squash court. That building now serves as the maintenance center for the park. Just north of this center is a large greenhouse that is open to the public. The grounds are magnificent, and include large formal gardens, a rock garden with a rushing brook, and a huge pergola whose fluted columns are almost hidden by a vast growth of wisteria and fox grape. There are flowers everywhere. Several gorgeous stands of tall beech trees grow among the acres of lawn that slope down to the shore.

The mansion itself, done in the Italian manner, has 42 rooms and is furnished opulently and tastefully, reflecting the wealth and sensitivity of the owners. Most of the furnishings were purchased during the Harkness' frequent trips to Europe and the Far East. Special note should be taken of the teak flooring, the wood paneling, and the graceful staircase. One can only stand in awe and wonder what it must have been like to live in this elegant house.

Another special feature of the house is the ongoing exhibits of bird paintings by Rex Brasher. Brasher, who spent most of his life in Kent, Conn., did not release his paintings for exhibit until, at age 51, he was satisfied that he had painted virtually every species of bird in North America. The state of Connecticut purchased the entire collection of more than 800 paintings and it is housed at the Harkness mansion. Because of space limitations, only about 200 of the paintings can be shown at any one time, but the exhibit is changed periodically.

In addition to the mansion and the greenhouse, the grounds are open to the public, and there are good picnic facilities. The lovely beach is closed to swimming, but fisherpersons are welcome to try their luck.

The park, located on Route 213 in Waterford, is open daily from 8 a.m. to sunset. The mansion is open daily from Memorial Day weekend through Labor Day and on weekends only through Columbus Day. The mansion hours are 10 a.m. to 5 p.m. on weekdays, and 10 a.m. to 7 p.m. on Saturdays. Sundays, and holidays. Admission to the park is $1 per car when the mansion is open; when the mansion is closed, admission to the park is free. Be sure to bring your camera.

Photo Courtesy of Connecticut Development Commission

Harkness Memorial State Park

Waterford

O'Neill Theater Center — This rapidly-growing and important theatrical center is now the home of the National Theater of the Deaf, the National Theater Institute, the National Playwrights Conference, the National Critics Institute, and many other groups involved with theater and television. One of the most important functions of the center is that of giving new playwrights a chance to have their plays performed or read. For example, the 1978 season saw 27 new works-in-progress performed during the regular July-August season.

Another function of the complex is to serve as a clearing house and bibliographical center of the works, letters, and other items having to do with Eugene O'Neill. To this end, the Monte Cristo Cottage on Pequot Avenue in New London has recently been purchased. Monte Cristo was the closest thing to a home that O'Neill ever had, and was the setting for several of his works, including "Long Day's Journey into Night." Plans are under way to turn the house into a museum of O'Neill memorabilia; it will also be the home of an important theatrical library. Renovations are in progress, but the cottage can be seen by appointment. Call Sally Pavetti at 203-443-5378.

The center is on Route 213 in Waterford, just down the road from Harkness Memorial State Park. For ticket and performance information, call 203-443-1238.

Jordan Schoolhouse and Beebe-Philips House — The Waterford Historical Society supports two building exhibits, both of which are located at the intersection of Routes 156 and 213 in Waterford. Originally built in 1740, the Jordan Schoolhouse is a very good example of the early one-room school. It is set up as a typical eighteenth-century school and will be of particular interest to children.

Next door to the schoolhouse is the Beebe-Philips House, a country house built in 1840. For many years, Waterford was the farming area which supplied New London with grain and produce, and this house, with its simple country furnishings, exemplifies the area's life-style in the mid-nineteenth century. Renovations are still in progress at presstime, but this house should be open to the public by the summer of 1979.

Both of these buildings are open from June 1 to October 1 on Sundays from 2 p.m. to 5 p.m. Admission is free.

Dining

★**Poor Richard's** — A blurb on Poor Richard's menu reads "This splendid Victorian eating house was conceived as a place of repose, superb dining, and fine drink in a charming setting of a bygone era. Five years of careful planning, building and acquisition of proper decor and furnishings were finally rewarded on our opening in April, 1977. The Chepping Dean Room and the Post Taverne on the first level were designed and furnished in the manner of an old English roadside pub. On the second level, the elegance and grandeur of the Victorian Era have been handsomely recaptured in the Drawing, Victoria, and Pen and Quill Rooms. Stained glass, imported long ago from England, France and Italy, but mostly from Early America, has been used lavishly throughout the restaurant to further enhance its elegant atmosphere."

Generally, when a restaurant toots its own horn, it's in the manner of a gross exaggeration; in Poor Richard's case, it's an understatement. This wonderful establishment occupies a large Victorian home that has been completely renovated and filled with mind-boggling objects. The tables are marble, the ceilings are made from 100-year-old cypress, and the walls are sheathed in copper. And there is stained glass everywhere. In fact, even if you're not hungry, stop in here just to see the windows and lamps, and be sure to spend some time in front of the "King's Crown," retrieved from a Newport mansion, which has over 2000 separate pieces of glass. Everything about the decor and atmosphere of this restaurant is perfect, and the hundreds of objects from all over the world blend in together beautifully. If there's such a thing as an ambience rating, Poor Richard's would get 100%.

But there's more: the food is outstanding! Every item on the menu, which includes poultry, fish, veal, and beef dishes, is excellent and exquisitely prepared in the continental manner. If you have only one meal to eat here, you *must* have either the bouillabaisse ($10.50) or any of the veal dishes ($8.95 to $9.25) which are absolutely super. The appetizers, soups, and desserts are equally good; but before you order, be aware that the helpings on the entrees are enormous. Dinner prices range from $7.95 to $10.95, but don't let your budget keep you away from this restaurant. At luncheon, you can select from a broad menu of sandwiches, beef and seafood entrees, or specialties, all from $1.95 to $4; and there is a good buffet at $3.95. But, again, if you're only here once, we have a strong recommendation: the poached eggs Bordelaise are fantastic.

Poor Richard's is located on Route 1 in Waterford, about two miles west of downtown New London and across the street from Waterford Shopping Center. Dinner is served between 5 p.m. and 10 p.m. on Monday through Thursday, 5 p.m. and 11 p.m. on Friday and Saturday, and 4 p.m. and 9:30 p.m. on Sunday. Luncheon is served between 11:30 a.m. and 2:30 p.m. Monday through Saturday. Sunday brunch is served from 11:30 a.m. to 3 p.m. Reservations are recommended. Credit cards: AE, BA/V, MC. 203-443-1813.

Photo Courtesy of O'Neill Theater Center

O'Neill Theater Center

East Lyme

(Including Black Point, Crescent Beach, Flanders, Giant's Neck Beach, and Niantic)

In 1665, East Lyme was a part of the large area on the eastern shore of the Connecticut River that separated from the Saybrook Colony and became known as the Town of Lyme. In 1816, East Lyme broke away from the huge town to incorporate independently. A fairly sizable section of East Lyme was won in a fistfight (see Old Lyme). The inland section of the town was mostly rural with farming and lumbering activities. The coastal section, known as Niantic, was a shipping and shipbuilding center, and today is a very busy summer resort area.

One of the most charming stories coming down from the colonial years happened in 1647 in East Lyme. One of the early settlers, Jonathan Rudd, had decided to marry, and the young couple had posted their banns. The wedding was to take place in midwinter with the arrival of a magistrate from Hartford. A tremendous blizzard hit the area, and the magistrate could not get through the snow to perform the ceremony. The desperate couple, aware that Gov. John Winthrop of the Massachusetts Bay Colony was visiting New London, (which at the time was under the jurisdiction of Massachusetts), appealed to him to marry them. He consented to come, but could not cross the stream that was the dividing line between Massachusetts and Connecticut. Nor could the couple be married in Massachusetts. The problem was solved by having Gov. Winthrop perform the ceremony in a loud voice as he stood on the eastern shore, while the young couple exchanged their vows in the snow on the western shore. As a result of this marriage, the name of the stream was changed from Sunkapaug to Bride Brook, and the event is recorded on a stone marker a few feet east of the small stream crossing Route 156 just west of the entrance to Rocky Neck State Park.

Another colonial East Lyme story has Capt. Reinold Marvin riding up to the lady he had been courting and announcing from the saddle: "Betty, the Lord has commanded me to marry you." She replied, "The Lord's will be done." Betty was the daughter of Ensign Lee who added some rooms to the Thomas Lee House around 1690 primarily because he had 12 children and two rooms didn't seem to be quite adequate. He opposed his daughter's engagement to Capt. Marvin and made that objection quite plain. The determined couple posted their banns, which read:

> Reinold Marvin and Betty Lee
> Do intend to marry;
> And though her Dad opposèd be,
> They will no longer tarry.

The winters may have been harsh and the Indians bothersome, but one can certainly say that romance flourished in early East Lyme.

Things to see & do

Thomas Lee House — Originally a one-over-one house built by Thomas Lee in 1660, this is reputed to be the oldest wood-frame structure in Connecticut. The house remained in the Lee family for 250 years and, upon the death of the last descendant at the beginning of the twentieth century, the home was purchased by the East Lyme Historical Society to prevent its demolition. The fascinating thing is that there was very little to restore: extensive repairs were necessary, but the house was architecturally intact. And the place is a dandy!

All of its architectural elements are original, from the wood paneling and fireplaces to the beams and flooring. Nothing is new or replaced, and in no other house in the area does the past come alive more than it does here. The furnishings are mostly from the period or earlier, and range from the rare to the priceless. Among the treasures are a chair, a large press chest, a hope chest, and a spice rack—all from the 1540s. How about a hobby horse carved in 1670? Every room is a treat, the kitchen especially so, with many rare early utensils and equipment. (Don't miss a look up the chimney in the kitchen.)

On the grounds of the Lee House is the Little Boston School, built in 1734. It operated continuously until 1922 and was subsequently purchased by the East Lyme Historical Society and moved here. The Society has not attempted to restore the building to its 1734 condition, but rather has chosen to show how the school was set up at the end of the nineteenth century. A tour of the school is included as a part of the tour of the Lee House.

Photo Courtesy of Connecticut Development Commission

Little Boston School: Thomas Lee House

53

The Thomas Lee House is located on Route 156 (take Exit 72 from I-95) just east of Rocky Neck State Park. The building is open daily, except Tuesdays, from Memorial Day through October 12 from 10 a.m. to 5 p.m. Admission is $1 for adults and 50¢ for children. If you have only a limited amount of time in the area, make sure this is one of your stops. And, try to have Mr. Manken as your tour guide: he's one of the best in the business.

Smith-Harris House — If you've had enough of driving and want an unusual place to eat that picnic lunch, give the Smith-Harris house a try. Owned by the Town of East Lyme, this house was built in 1838 on 100 acres of land, and was a working farm for over a century. There is nothing fancy or unusual about the house, and that's part of its charm: it's just what it was, a plain farmhouse from the mid-nineteenth century. In many ways this simple house will be educational for children who have been dragged through some of the ancient homes in the area and "can't imagine how anyone could have lived that way." This house provides a bridge between the past and the present. Restoration is in progress, and the long-range plan for the property is to return it to a working farm that will be open to the public. There are picnic tables and lots of trees.

To reach the house, take Exit 73 from I-95 and turn east on Society Road. After three-quarters of a mile, the driveway will be on your left just before the junior high school. The house is open in the summer daily, except Thursdays, from 1 p.m. to 5 p.m. and in the winter on weekends only from 1 p.m. to 5 p.m. There is no admission charge.

Rocky Neck State Park — Located on Route 156 near Exit 72 of I-95, Rocky Neck is a large well-run state park that offers many comfortable campsites for travelers, and picnic and swimming facilities for the day visitor. One unusual feature here is a number of picnic tables lining the shore and providing visitors with a fine view of Long Island Sound. There is a large, handsome pavilion on the hill overlooking the beach that offers the usual facilities and concessions. The beach is not overly large, but it's pretty, with sufficient room to allow for some degree of privacy and peace. Fishing and exploring can be enjoyed from the breakwater at the west end of the beach. Campers should make reservations.

Dining

Black Whale — If you are looking for a great Italian meal at a reasonable price, the Black Whale Restaurant is a good bet. It is small and fairly intimate, and if it's chilly, a fire in the dining room fireplace will be lit. On Friday and Saturday nights, soft piano music complements the meal.

A wide variety of Italian specialties from fettucini Alfredo to homemade cheese manicotti can be ordered at an average price of about $5.50. In addition, steaks, chops, chicken, seafood, and veal are available at about $6.00. The veal is very good: try either the veal piccata or the veal pizzaiola. The Italian sauce is real, not your basic stuff out of a jar, and if you have never had the pleasure of eating homemade pasta, you're in for a treat: Hazel Campanella, the owner, makes her own. Children may select not only the usual chicken and hamburger, but are offered veal and fish too, all in the $2.95 to $3.50 range. A broad luncheon menu includes just about everything and carries an average price tag of about $2.75. If you're in the area near Rocky Neck State Park, or want to have a fine Italian meal, give this restaurant a try: you'll never forget their hot garlic bread.

To get there, take Exit 72 off I-95 and turn right on Route 156. It is about 3 miles west of Niantic on Route 156 and near the entrance to Rocky Neck. The Black Whale is open from 11:30 a.m. to 1 a.m. daily except Tuesdays. Reservations are suggested, especially on summer weekends. Credit cards: AE, BA/V, MC. 203-739-7382.

Chopping Block — Every once in a while, you stumble across a restaurant that has one item on the menu that brings you back time and again. The Chopping Block is one of these, and their specialty is prime rib. In dimly lit, rustic surroundings, hungry meat-eaters gather in droves and, we must assume, go away satiated and happy.

From a menu very similar to the Chart House or Chuck's, the prime rib stands out and is the main reason you should eat here. For $9.95 (which includes a trip to a good salad bar) the waiter will bring you an absolutely huge slab of tender, perfectly done, beef. Weighing between 30 oz. and 35 oz., this is the biggest piece of meat you'll find anywhere around. The other items on the menu (steak, chicken, and seafood) are perfectly fine, but when you go to the Chopping Block, order the prime rib, and bring an empty stomach (and/or a big dog).

This restaurant is located on Route 161 about 3 miles north of Exit 74 of I-95, and is found on the grounds of the Ponderosa Campground. They are open seven days a week for dinner only between 5 p.m. and 10 p.m. The Chopping Block does not accept reservations, so in the summer and on weekends, expect a wait (sometimes up to an hour, but it's worth it). Credit cards: BA/V, MC. 203-739-5515.

Photo Courtesy of Connecticut Development Commission

Florence Griswold House (Old Lyme)

Old Lyme

(Including Black Hall, Laysville, Sound View, and South Lyme)

In 1645, George Fenwick of the Saybrook Colony granted some land on the east side of the Connecticut River to Matthew Griswold and the settlement of that wilderness area began. The section, which included what are now Old Lyme, Lyme, and East Lyme was known as East Saybrook. It was officially separated from the Saybrook Colony in 1665 with the signing of an agreement known as "The Loving Parting." In 1885, the northern and southern sections of the town split, the northern section retaining the name of Lyme, and the more populous southern area calling itself Old Lyme.

Of all the towns on the Connecticut shore, Old Lyme has, more than most, preserved its traditions of culture, public spirit, and residential peace. The town has produced many notable men including two Governors, several generals, a Chief Justice of the Supreme Court, as well as many diplomats and sea captains. Except for a flourishing business in the building and sailing of ships during the eighteenth and nineteenth centuries, there has been literally no significant commercial enterprise in the town during its long history.

One of the less peaceful but typically creative moments in the history of Old Lyme concerned a longstanding dispute with New London about a four-mile-wide strip of land. It was finally decided to "leave it to the Lord," and a bareknuckle fight was arranged between champions of the two towns. The fight went to the Lord; the land went to Old Lyme.

In the early part of the twentieth century, Old Lyme gained fame as an art colony when Florence Griswold opened her hearth and home to artists from all over the country. Her interest in the arts and her gentle encouragement, combined with the pastoral peace of the land, soon made the town a Mecca for both the well-known and the unknown artist. Art still plays a major role in Old Lyme, and there are excellent exhibits at the Florence Griswold House and the gallery of the Lyme Art Association.

Things to see & do

One of the most notable physical features of Old Lyme is its extensive marshland, and you can get a good look at some of it by taking Smith Neck Road (off Route 156, one and one-half miles south of I-95) to the Great Island Wildlife Area. This is a popular boat launching site, and the views of the salt marshes and the mouth of the Connecticut River with its lighthouses are superb. During the summer, with binoculars, one can spot several pairs of nesting ospreys (yes, they're back!) on man-made perches deep in the marsh. Even better, if you're carrying some sort of shallow draft boat, you can get out on the miles of tidal rivers and see a wide variety of water birds. (If you see what looks like a grouchy old man trying to stare you down, it's a black-crowned night heron.) A restricted beach area just south of Smith Neck, accessible only by boat, has been set aside for nesting terns.

Another characteristic of Old Lyme is its gracious old homes. Take Lyme Street north from the Congregational Church. This wide, quiet road has many beautiful houses, not the least of which is the Florence Griswold House.

Florence Griswold House — The advent of steam-powered boats in the latter part of the nineteenth century caused certain hardships on those who made their living from sailing, and the family of Capt. Robert Griswold was no exception. After his death in 1884, his widow and daughters, in order to keep their home, turned the house into a finishing school for women. By 1901, the school had been discontinued, and only Florence Griswold, one of the captain's daughters, was left in the house. Her friendship with some New York artists prompted her to turn her home into a boardinghouse for artists. It was to become one of the most famous art colonies in the country.

The house, built in 1817, is spectacular, reflecting the taste, formality, and prosperity of early Old Lyme. During the period that the house served as a retreat for artists (from 1901 to

1936), the citizens of Old Lyme were often critical of the hijinks and pranks of the artists, but they never failed to show up at any of the art exhibitions. After her death in 1936, the artists formed the Florence Griswold Association to maintain her house as a museum of history and art. In 1955, the Lyme Historical Society joined with the association and made the house their headquarters.

And thank heavens they kept the house open to the public! Many of the door panels and walls are covered with beautiful paintings done by the resident artists, sometimes in lieu of rent. (One art-loving visitor offered to buy a door panel; when refused, he offered to buy the door. Again refused, he tried to buy the house, which thankfully is not for sale.) The rear room served as a dining room for the artists, and the walls are almost completely covered with wonderful paintings. One particularly interesting piece is a panel above the fireplace on which they painted a caricature of themselves depicting their personalities and fellowship.

Besides the paintings, which seem to be everywhere, there are exhibits of tools, photographs, and early documents in several rooms. One room on the second floor has a marvelous display of Victorian toys.

American Impressionism had its start in this house, as well as the American application of the Barbizon style. Anyone who has the slightest interest in art and art history should visit this special place.

The Florence Griswold House is located on Lyme Street, next door to the Lyme Art Association and across the street from the Old Lyme Inn. The house is open daily (except Monday) in the summer from 10 a.m. to 5 p.m., Sundays from 1 p.m. to 5 p.m. In the winter, the house is open from 1 p.m. to 5 p.m. on Wednesdays, Thursdays, Fridays, and Sundays. Admission is free, but donations are appreciated.

Lyme Art Association — When the artists at "Miss Florence's" had attained some degree of success and had outgrown the public library for their exhibits, they decided to open their own gallery. Florence Griswold donated the land, and the building was erected in 1922. This art gallery has the distinction of being the first one known to have been built and financed by the artists themselves.

Old Lyme

There are three shows each season, and most of the objects are for sale. On display are pieces of sculpture, oils, water-colors, and pastels. For those who are either tired of modern art or can't stand it, this fine gallery would be enjoyable; every-thing on display here is "realistic" and consists mostly of land-scapes, still-lifes, and portraits, all of them very good.

Located on Lyme Street across from the Old Lyme Inn, the gallery is open from the last week in May through the middle of September, daily from 10 a.m. to 5 p.m. except Sunday, when the hours are 1 p.m. to 5 p.m. Admission is 50¢.

Nut Museum — "Oh, nobody ever thinks about nuts. Nuts can be so beautiful if looked aright. Take some home and handle them properly, artistically and feel a new taste being born." So goes the first stanza of the nut anthem, "Nuts Are Beautiful," and the inspiration for curator Elizabeth Tashjian's latest project: a sculpture garden with five huge aluminum pieces on the grounds of Elya, her sprawling nineteenth-century mansion. One wing of the house is devoted to the display of nuts from all over the world as well as nut jewelry, furni-ture, and collages. Ms. Tashjian has also filled the rooms with her nut art and masks. If you're lucky, you will hear her sing not only the nut anthem, but also her special composition for children, "The March of the Nuts."

If all this sounds a little nutty to you, you only have to spend some time with this exuberant and enthusiastic curator to see that this collection is one of the most special and erudite in the world. To Ms. Tashjian, every nut represents a philosophical idea. For example, the 35-pound Coco de Mer nut (which is not only the largest nut in the world, but has to be one of the most sensual things produced by nature) has prompted Ms. Tashjian to challenge not only the story of Adam and Eve, but to take on Darwin as well. In this museum even the lowly filbert rises to unimagined cultural and artistic heights.

The large collection of nutcrackers seems somewhat out of place, but "although they are the historical enemy of nuts," Ms. Tashjian says, "here in this place they can live side by side in peaceful contentment." (The nutcrackers can certainly live more peacefully than many of the nut exhibits which are periodically raided by squirrels and chipmunks.) However you

60

may feel about your visit to this wonderful and nutty place, we can guarantee that you will come away with a changed attitude towards our hard-shelled friends.

The museum can be reached by taking the first right (Ferry Road) off Route 156 south of I-95. Just look for a 10-foot aluminum nutcracker hanging from a tree and turn in. The museum is open from May to November on Wednesdays, Saturdays, and Sundays from 2 p.m. to 5 p.m. Admission is one nut (important) and one buck. Have fun.

Dining

★**Old Lyme Inn** — It is appropriate that a graceful, wealthy town like Old Lyme should have a first-class French restaurant. The surroundings in this fine restaurant are gracious: a single candle and rosebud adorn each of the large widely-spaced tables, and the soft lighting, comfortable chairs, and friendly waiters soon put you at an ease you never thought possible. This is a relaxed, opulent place that serves what has to be the finest French food in the region. Be prepared to pay New York prices, but it's worth every penny of it. This is truly a great restaurant, and our personal favorite of favorites.

Choosing among the four or five appetizers is a real chore, but the Irish smoked salmon and the spinach quiche with goat cheese are outstanding. The soups are wonderful too, and, if they have it, be sure to order the fantastic cream of mushroom soup made with morels. Between six and eight entrees are available and usually include a selection of chicken, fish, beef, pork, lamb, and veal dishes, all of which are carefully and beautifully prepared and are enhanced by some of the most incredible sauces you'll ever have. Any of the fish dishes are superb, and the veal is not to be believed. Entree prices range between $8 and $12.50. For the final culinary coup, if you still have room, a dessert cart filled with luscious cakes and pastries will be wheeled to your table. Our favorite time to go to the Old Lyme Inn is on winter weeknights when new and exotic dishes are prepared and tested. Luncheons here are equally as good as dinner. The menu offers six to eight interesting French entrees from $3.50 to $6. The Old Lyme Inn

Old Lyme

is a gentle, wonderful place with absolutely superb food. The inn is located on Lyme Street directly across the street from the Lyme Art Association; from I-95, take Exit 70. Luncheon is served from noon to 2 p.m. Tuesday through Saturday. Dinner is served from 6 p.m. to 8:30 p.m. Tuesday through Thursday, 6 p.m. to 9:15 p.m. Friday and Saturday, and 1 p.m. to 8 p.m. on Sunday. The restaurant is closed on Mondays. Jackets are required after 6 p.m. Reservations are recommended. Credit cards: AE, BA/V, CB, MC. 203-434-2600.

Bee and Thistle Inn — The Bee and Thistle, one of New England's classic-type inns, occupies a grand old home originally built in 1756. Here you may have an informal, relaxed meal in a setting very much like a private home. There are several small, well-appointed dining rooms where one never realizes that about 60 other people are being fed at the same time. One of the great treats about a meal here is innkeeper Barbara Bellows going from room to room singing ballads while accompanying herself on dulcimer or guitar. This is a very special place for that very special occasion.

The menu is extremely limited, but everything offered is excellent. The entrees are a fresh fish dish, a shrimp dish, Veal Viennese, a New York sirloin, and a chicken dish. The cooking, done with care and imagination by Gene Bellows, is primarily American with a European influence. It is unusual and it is very good. Everything is fresh and all the cooking is done on the premises. Prices for the entrees average about $8.50 and include bread, a colorful salad, and vegetables. For appetizers, there are two soups and a melon cup, and for dessert four treats are offered; if they have it, order their wonderful home-made pie at $1.25.

As we go to press, the Bee and Thistle is locked in a legal battle concerning their application for a liquor license. So, when you call, find out if it's been resolved. In the meantime, bring your own beverage; they provide the setups.

The Bee and Thistle Inn is located on Lyme Street and is the first building north of the Florence Griswold House. They are open for dinner only, from 6 p.m. to 9 p.m. Wednesday through Sunday; closed on Monday and Tuesday. Reservations are recommended. Credit cards: BA/V, DC. 203-434-1667.

Lyme

(Including Hadlyme, Hamburg, and North Lyme)

Once a part of the huge town of Lyme (including what is now Lyme, Old Lyme, and East Lyme), this sparsely-populated rural area ended up with the original name, while most of the early history of the town occurred in what is now Old Lyme. Route 156 traverses Lyme, south to north, and is a truly lovely drive that gives the flavor of the town today: a peaceful place of woods and meadows bordering an almost completely undeveloped section of the Connecticut River. The hamlet of Hamburg is worth stopping in, as the surrounding countryside and the cove are beautiful, making it a favorite mooring place for cruising boats. Formerly a farming and lumbering area, present-day Lyme has virtually no industry; less than 2000 lucky people live here and enjoy a rare form of peace and contentment.

Things to see & do

Gillette Castle State Park — If you had scads of money, odd tastes, and plenty of time, you too could build something like Gillette Castle. William Gillette, the noted nineteenth-century actor who adapted the role of Sherlock Holmes for himself and gave more than 13,000 performances, had just about decided to build the house of his dreams on Long Island.

A short time before construction was to begin, he took a cruise up the Connecticut River on his 144-foot houseboat, *Aunt Polly*. Mooring on the eastern shore just below a lovely set of hills known as "The Seven Sisters," he fell in love with the area, and made up his mind on the spot to build his house right there.

Within several weeks, he had purchased 122 acres along the shore and had selected the highest point on the hills as the site for the house. To get workers and materials to the site, he designed and built a railroad. (Gillette was an inveterate railroad nut; he was to extend the rails all through the property so that he might be the engineer not only on solo journeys, but to provide his many guests with a rare form of entertainment.) Sadly, the tracks today are gone. All that remains of Gillette's wonderful hobby are a few broken-down trestles. Construction of the house took five years (from 1914 to 1919), and Gillette, then in his sixties, oversaw every detail. Evidence of his brilliance and eccentricity can be found everywhere.

Don't get the idea that this house is a copy of some European castle; this place is unique and is nothing more than the product of Gillette's far-ranging mind. The granite walls, which are in places four to five feet thick, tower over the river like some giant's sandcastle, or, more accurately, like the fortress of some mad genius. Of the 24 oddly-shaped rooms, no two are alike, nor does there seem to be any sort of architectural logic in their layout. Gillette not only designed the Castle, but most of the furniture as well; almost all of it is made from hand-hewn oak. Many pieces are built into the walls or set up on movable tracks. He even designed the light fixtures. The doors are a special treat. Made of heavy oak, many of them are intricately carved and have a wooden-latch arrangement of such complexity that it's a wonder any of them ever got opened.

The main part of the first floor is an enormous living room with an overhanging balcony. Just off the living room is a greenhouse, complete with fountains and pools. Theater buffs will enjoy the third floor, which has several rooms devoted to Gillette's memorabilia, including a complete stage set from his Sherlock Holmes play. Another room houses part of his rather fine art collection. There is even a room paying homage to his beloved houseboat, which sank in 1932. (There is a persistent story that the owner himself blew it up over a tax dispute with

Photo Courtesy of Connecticut Department of Commerce

Gillette Castle

the town of Lyme.) Indeed, everywhere one wanders in this remarkable castle, the personality of William Gillette is ever-present.

Gillette died in 1937 at the age of 87. In his will, he commanded his executors to make sure that "the property did not fall into the hands of some blithering saphead." But not many people wanted it, and when it came on the market, the high bid was a mere $35,000. In 1943, the State acquired the property, which today is one of the most popular attractions in Connecticut.

There's a lot more to the park than just the castle. The forest is lush and has many ancient pine trees; several well-marked hiking trails wind through the woods. There are a few picnic areas, the most popular of which is "Grand Central Station," the old terminal for Gillette's railroad. And there are wide stone patios located on the river side of the house that provide the best view of the river and valley around.

Gillette Castle is at once ugly and beautiful, strange and wonderful. Go see for yourself.

The park can be reached by taking the Chester-Hadlyme Ferry on Route 148 or by crossing the East Haddam Bridge (Route 82) near Exit 7 on Route 9. Until the access road is improved and the parking area enlarged, be prepared for a small traffic jam, especially on weekends. The castle is open from Memorial Day to Columbus Day, daily from 11 a.m. to 5 p.m. Admission is 50¢ for adults; children under 12 are admitted free. There is no admission fee to the park itself, which is open year-round during daylight hours.

Chester-Hadlyme Ferry — The eastern landing of the Chester-Hadlyme Ferry is found at the foot of Route 148 near Gillette Castle. For details, refer to Chester.

Nehantic State Park — This park is found off Route 156, three and one-half miles north of I-95. It is largely undeveloped and has two lovely lakes, Norwich Pond and Uncas Lake. Norwich Pond is the smaller of the two with a good boat-launching site that can also be used for swimming. Uncas Lake is much larger and also has a fine launching area. In addition, there is a beach and picnic area that can be reached by taking the first right on the Norwich Pond cut-off. The fishing is reported to be excellent, but for those who are getting ready to crank up the old Evinrude, take note that no motors of any kind are allowed on the lakes. This is a place of beauty and peace, and it's nice to know that it will stay that way for a while. Take a canoe and picnic lunch, and enjoy this quiet, uncrowded park.

East Haddam

(Including Bashan, Little Haddam, Millington, Moodus, and North Plain)

Originally a part of Haddam (across the river), this area was called Machimoodus ("a place of noises") by the Indians. In the early 1670s, settlement had begun, and by 1685 a number of families had moved across the river. As was the case in many of the early coastal towns, the new settlers had a difficult time getting to and from church services and meetings, and this difficulty was compounded in East Haddam's case by the Connecticut River, which was almost impossible to cross in winter. As early as 1697, the residents on the eastern shore petitioned for a separate church. This petition was finally granted in 1700 with the establishment of the East Haddam Society. In 1734, the towns split up, and East Haddam incorporated as an independent town.

Shipping and shipbuilding were important early industries. In addition, for a time, East Haddam had thriving shad and salmon businesses. During the 1870s, the town was a well-known summer resort with visitors coming from as far away as New York and Philadelphia. Today, East Haddam is primarily residential, with the woods and meadows of this large town contributing to its rural quality. The strange noises noticed by the Indians are still heard from time to time and are believed to be of geological origin.

Things to see & do

Goodspeed Opera House — William H. Goodspeed was an
ambitious and hard-working individual who would probably
prefer to be remembered as a wealthy and dynamic business-
man instead of a person who built an opera house. Born in
1816, Goodspeed early on decided that he could own East
Haddam if he so chose: he eventually owned or operated a
hotel, a bank, the general store, the river ferry, a railroad line,
a steamboat line, a shipyard, and the opera house.

In the mid-1800s, East Haddam was a popular summer
resort with many of the visitors arriving by steamer. At that
point, the town had two landings, the Upper and the Lower.
The Lower Landing was Goodspeed's and was considered the
less fashionable of the two for several reasons, including the
fact that the folks who stayed at the Upper Landing sometimes
had access to plays at nearby Maple Seminary. Goodspeed was
a man who was seldom outdone, so he set about to build a
rival attraction in the form of an opera house. He was also
a very practical man, so when he designed the building he

Photo By Mary Alice McAlpin

Goodspeed Opera House

consolidated several of his businesses right on the premises. The basement on the river level became the passenger and freight terminal for his steamboat business. The first floor housed the general store, and the second floor contained offices, which were rented out to local businessmen. The top two floors were the Goodspeed Opera House.

Construction began early in 1876. The building took 18 months to complete, and the first performance was given on Oct. 24, 1877. Goodspeed spared no expense or effort to bring the best shows and performers to his opera house and the theater flourished. Following his death in 1882, the opera house went into a long period of decline, ending with the professional performances in 1902.

During World War I, the building housed a Connecticut militia unit, which was there to guard the East Haddam Bridge from sabotage. In the 1930s, the building served only as a warehouse for local merchants, and by 1943, when the property was purchased by the state, the once-proud building was turned into a state highway garage. Ten years later, needing larger and more modern quarters, the Highway Department was considering demolishing the building and erecting a new garage on the site. When rumors of this project spread, concerned citizens began organizing, and after years of hard work and appeals to the General Assembly and the Governor, the building was sold in 1959 to the newly-formed Goodspeed Opera House Foundation for the sum of one dollar. After several more years of fund raising and architectural research, reconstruction was ready to begin. The grand opening of the completely restored opera house took place on June 18, 1963, and it has been a successful theater ever since.

This place is a gem. The enormous building (it is the tallest wooden structure on the 400 miles of the Connecticut River) has been beautifully restored to its original ornate Victorian state. There is a large curving bar and "ladies parlor" straight out of the late nineteenth century, and drinkers can stroll out to a porch overlooking the river. The lobby has an antique popcorn machine which hums merrily at each performance. This splendid opera house is one of the most beautiful small theaters in the country. The renovations were accurate and complete, and the theater is decked out as it was—with the rococo flourish of a riverboat saloon. The central staircase is so elegant that many women attending performances wear long dresses just so they can descend these stairs and get a feeling for graceful times long gone.

Each season three musical comedies are presented: two revivals and one new show. Among the shows that had their start at Goodspeed's are *Man of La Mancha, Shenandoah,* and *Annie.* The season runs from mid-April to mid-November. In the winter, a travel series is presented on occasional weekends.

The Goodspeed Opera House is located at the eastern end of the East Haddam Bridge (Route 82) which, incidentally, is the longest swing bridge in the United States. Tours of the opera house are held on Mondays (except holidays) during July and August from 1 p.m. to 3 p.m. There is a nominal admission charge. For performance and ticket information, call 203-873-8668.

Nathan Hale Schoolhouse — Walking up the hill to this tiny schoolhouse, one can imagine what it must have been like to attend school in the eighteenth century. Nathan Hale taught here during the winter of 1773-74, and the building, which is beautifully preserved, is set up exactly as it was in those days. While the setting is stern and sparse, it's obvious that much learning went on here. This charming building on a hilltop is well worth a stop. Near the school is the grave of Maj. Gen. Joseph Spencer, one of East Haddam's most famous citizens.

The Nathan Hale Schoolhouse is open during the summer on weekends and holidays from 2 p.m. to 4 p.m. Admission is 25¢ for adults; children are admitted free. Follow Route 149 about 200 yards north of the intersection with Route 82. The parking area is on the left.

St. Stephen's Bell — While you're parked at the lot of the Nathan Hale Schoolhouse, wander north about 200 feet, and you will see what is probably the oldest bell in North America. The bell, which hangs in the belfry of St. Stephen's Episcopal Church, has a rather interesting history. According to tradition, the bell was cast for a Spanish monastery in 815 A.D. When Napoleon invaded Spain, the monastery was destroyed, and the bell was left behind in the rubble. In 1834, needing some heavy items for ballast for the return trip to America, a Yankee sea captain loaded it on board and brought it to New York. There, a ship chandler whose wife was from East Haddam, bought it and promptly had it shipped to St. Stephen's, where a bell was needed. You may be able to find someone around to let you into the belfry for a close look.

East Haddam Historical Society Museum — Still in the development stages as we go to press, the East Haddam Historical Society Museum hopes to open sometime during the summer of 1979. It is planned that the bulk of the collection will consist of photographs, both old and new, of the town and the surrounding area. In addition, there will be a Colonial Room and a Victorian Room, each displaying furniture, clothes, and artifacts of the periods. Also, pieces from an early silver factory in East Haddam will be on display. The museum is located on Route 149 just north of the intersection with Route 82 (on the way to the Nathan Hale Schoolhouse).

Amasa Day House — Built in 1816, the Amasa Day House is a fine example of Connecticut country architecture in the early 1800s. The house is owned and maintained by the Antiquarian and Landmarks Society of Connecticut and features seven museum rooms, each tastefully restored with appropriate period colors and fabrics. One of the unusual and rare features of the house is original stenciling that can be seen in two first floor rooms, on the front stairs, and in the upstairs hall. There are particularly good collections of children's toys, clocks, mirrors, ceramics, and wrought iron. The furnishings, which are quite splendid, are mostly from the early 1800s. This house is well worth the drive.

Located at the junction of Routes 149 and 151 on the green in Moodus, the Amasa Day House is open from May 15 to October 15, daily from 1 p.m. to 5 p.m. Admission is 75¢ for adults and 25¢ for those under 16.

Devil's Hopyard State Park — This lovely park is way out in the boonies, but if a rushing stream, waterfalls, and big trees are your thing, this would be the place to go. The park runs along Eight Mile River and offers some good hiking trails, the most popular of which lead to the beautiful Chapman Upper and Lower Falls. There are some nice picnic facilities along the river, but swimming is prohibited. The unusual name of the park came from an old legend, which had the devil sitting atop Chapman Falls directing witches who would stir an evil mixture containing hops in the potholes at the foot of the falls. One might guess from a look in the trash cans that another type of evil brew made from hops is being consumed on the premises these days.

To reach the park from East Haddam, take Route 82 east and follow the signs. When you leave the park, if you're heading for the coast, be sure to take the road that follows the Eight Mile River; this is as close to Vermont as you can get in Connecticut and is one of the loveliest drives in the state.

Dining

Gelston House — The Gelston House has been a licensed tavern since 1736 and through all these years it has acquired, among other treasures, a chandelier from the Aga Khan Palace in India and an exquisite silver roast beef cart that once served King Carol of Rumania. There are several dining rooms including a grand Victorian room and a large sunny Greenhouse with a wonderful view of the Connecticut River. Anyone attending a Goodspeed performance can make the evening complete by dining here.

After having any one of their fabulous appetizers (fabulous but expensive), diners can select from a menu featuring veal, roast duckling, and baked stuffed shrimp as well as a large selection of fish and beef dishes. The chicken Kiev ($6.25) and the lamb shish kebab ($6.95) are particularly outstanding among the lower priced entrees. The average entree is about $8.00 and the portions are huge. Luncheon offerings include an assortment of sandwiches and salads, but *always* ask about the special: nearly always superb at about $3.50. All in all, Gelston House is an opulent and fun place with very good food.

Located right next door to the Goodspeed Opera House, this restaurant is open from 11:30 a.m. to 2 p.m. and from 5:30 p.m. to 9 p.m. every Tuesday through Friday; from 11:30 a.m. to 2 p.m. and from 5 p.m. to 10 p.m. on Saturday, and from noon to 8 p.m. on Sunday. It is closed on Monday. Reservations are recommended, especially during the Goodspeed season. Credit cards: AE, BA/V, DC, MC. 203-873-9300 or 203-873-8257.

Chester

Originally, Chester was a part of the Saybrook Colony, and when that plantation was "quartered" in 1648, the area that is now Chester was called the Pataconk Quarter. Pataconk was an Indian word meaning "sweating place," a place where ailing members of the tribe were placed on hot stones and covered with blankets. Steam was produced by throwing water on the stones and, when it was deemed that the patient had had enough, he was dunked in the river—kind of a primitive sauna. The area was first settled in 1692; in 1740, the General Assembly made Pataconk a separate community known as the Fourth Ecclesiastical Society of Saybrook, to be called Chester. In 1836, Chester incorporated as an independent town.

During the eighteenth and nineteenth centuries, there were many small industries in the town including shipbuilding, quarrying, and milling, as well as several factories manufacturing axe handles, gimlets (the tool, not the drink), and ink stands. Did you know that Samuel Silliman (who was known as "the Father of the Modern Inkwell") was a native of Chester? Today, Chester is a pretty and peaceful little town situated on what is probably the most handsome section of the Connecticut River.

Things to see & do

In the center of Chester is what has to be the most imposing liquor store in the state. We won't say any more about it here; you'll have to go see for yourself. To reach the Old Meeting House, take Water Street a short way out of the center and bear right on Goose Hill Road. Now a community center, this building has been in public use since 1793. If you're a movie buff, you'll be interested to learn that this meeting house (as well as the rest of Chester) played a major role in "It Happened to Jane" with Doris Day and Jack Lemmon. Across the street from this building are two fine old cemeteries with lots of interesting early headstones.

Photo Courtesy of Connecticut Department of Commerce

Chester-Hadlyme Ferry

Chester-Hadlyme Ferry — If you're heading for Gillette Castle and have some time, consider taking the ferry across the river. To reach the ferry landing, take Route 9A north of Chester and turn right on Route 148. This ferry is the second oldest in Connecticut, having been in operation since 1769. The boat is small and can only take a few cars at a time, but except for summer weekends, the wait is worth it. There are spectacular views of the Connecticut River during the five-minute crossing, and the Chester landing affords a great look at William Gillette's bizarre house.

The ferry operates daily during daylight hours from April 1 to November 1. The fare is 25¢ for car and driver plus 5¢ for each additional passenger.

Cedar Lake — This attractive lake may be reached by taking Route 148 west from the Chester town center. The lake offers swimming, boating, fishing, and picnicking. There is a $2 daily charge per family with seasonal passes available. The boat-launch area is at the corner of Cedar Lake Road on the western edge of the lake. The fishing is reported to be excellent, with an active ongoing stocking program.

Cockaponset State Forest — Part of this sprawling state forest reaches into the western section of Chester. An entrance and parking area can be found by going north about two and one-half miles on Cedar Lake Road (see above). There are some hiking trails, but most of the activity in this area of the park takes place around Pataconk Lake, which has swimming, fishing, and picnic facilities.

Dining

★**Chart House** — The restoration and revitalization of any old or unique building is something that should always be applauded. When, as a part of that revitalization, an absolutely top-drawer restaurant is included, the applause should turn into cheers and hosannas. The Rogers and Champion Brushworks, established in 1859 and devoted to the manufacture of brooms and brushes, was only one of many manufacturers in the area to use water power to drive its machines. Now this factory, the only one still standing, is the home of the Chart House Restaurant, a place where you will have an excellent and comfortable meal.

The entrance to the Chart House is a narrow covered bridge traversing a rushing stream and a dramatic waterfall; the only thing that's missing here is a churning waterwheel. Once inside, the low ceilings, the original lights, windows, and chestnut beams, and the subdued decor suggest that you're going to have a very pleasant evening. Much of the original manufacturing paraphernalia is still in place: the gears and belts and flywheels that helped turn out the brushes for many decades. Even the bell, placed in 1886, that was used to call the workers (and in World War II was used as an air raid signal), is still there. A meal here is a pleasant trip into the past and an interesting look at the ingenuity of early entrepreneurs.

And then there's the food: a limited selection of excellent dishes. The Chart House is a nationwide chain known for its fine food and good service, and this particular establishment is no exception. For a fairly reasonable price, you can have an enormous salad (their house dressing is unbelievable), all the hot bread you can eat, and a choice of steaks, prime ribs, fish, scallops, or chicken breast. The helpings are large. For example, there are two sizes of prime rib, the larger of which (the Callahan Cut at $11.45) weighs in at 24 oz. The teriyaki chicken breast (which is filling and delicious) is the lowest-priced item at $5.95. A secret for our readers: if you want a great steak and like it cooked rare or medium rare, always ask if a "baseball" is available. It's not on the menu, but it's the same price as the top sirloin ($7.95) and is as close to a filet mignon as you can get without calling it that; they always have a few in the kitchen. The dessert selection is limited, but that doesn't matter: anyone with any sense orders their unforgettable mud pie. The Chart House, all things considered, is one of the best restaurants around.

Located right at the end of the exit ramp of Exit 6 of Route 9 (about 8 miles north of Old Saybrook), the Chart House serves dinner only and is open from 5:30 p.m. to 10 p.m. Monday through Thursday, 5:30 p.m. to 11 p.m. on Friday and Saturday, and noon to 9 p.m. on Sunday. Reservations are recommended. Credit cards: AE, BA/V, DC, MC. 203-526-9898.

Deep River

(Including Winthrop)

Deep River is the last remnant of the Saybrook Colony and was known as Saybrook until 1947. Despite the fact that Deep River was not an established settlement until well over a century after the founding of the Colony, the secession (between 1836 and 1852) of Chester, Westbrook, Essex, and Old Saybrook from the Colony left Saybrook (Deep River) with the original name and all the Colony's records dating back to 1666.

Because the town was late in being settled, there are not as many ancient houses in Deep River as in other coastal or down-river towns. But, like many of her neighbors, Deep River had a flourishing shipbuilding industry, and the town produced several notable sea captains. Another early industry was the manufacture of handmade ivory combs, a business begun in the 1700s. The product proved a success and, with typical Yankee ingenuity and the use of water power to drive the machines, the ivory industry thrived. In the 1800s, several separate factories in Deep River and Ivoryton were turning out various ivory products: collar buttons, chess sets, teething rings, billiard balls, combs, and other products. In 1839, the local companies started the cutting of piano keys out of ivory and soon thereafter applied themselves to the manufacture of piano and organ keyboards and actions. In the mid-1800s, several of these companies merged to form Pratt, Read and Company, which today is headquartered in Ivoryton and is the largest manufacturer of organ and piano keyboards and actions in the world. It is interesting to note that at one time the Deep River/Ivoryton area was known as the largest importer of ivory anywhere.

Present-day Deep River is a quiet town noted for the spacious lawns and grounds of its earlier homes. The town is nationally known for the Annual Ancient Muster of Fife and Drum Corps.

Things to see & do

Annual Ancient Muster of Fife and Drum Corps — On the third Saturday of each July, the quiet town of Deep River comes to noisy life when the Annual Muster is held. As many as one hundred different groups from all over the country and from as far away as Switzerland attract thousands of observers, the press, and national television. Dressed in uniforms of the Revolutionary War, the War of 1812, and the Civil War, the fife and drummers march in a parade to the grounds where each unit is given three minutes to exhibit their marching and musical styles. This is an event that has been taking place for over a century and is unmatched anywhere in the world. The Muster should not be missed, but have fun finding a parking space.

The Stone House — Located on South Main Street (Route 9A), this handsome home, now the headquarters of the Deep River Historical Society, was erected in 1840 by Deacon Ezra Southworth as a home for his bride. The stone used in its construction came from quarries owned by Deacon Southworth, and its architecture is truly representative of the period.

The Marine Room on the first floor is filled with interesting nautical items including oil paintings, early photographs, navigation instruments, and many unusual documents. The rest of the house is given over to exhibits from different periods, but there are several items that demand special attention. There is a fine collection of cut glass, made in Deep River at the turn of the century, showing the characteristic Deep River "butterfly." Two very special pieces of furniture, a piano and a bureau, were made from Connecticut's most famous tree, the Charter Oak. In the meeting room there is an unusual display of walking sticks from all over the world, and a fine exhibit of Indian artifacts. In the same room, and not to be missed, is a large display of ivory products, most of them coming from the factories that abounded in Deep River and Ivoryton during the 1800s.

The Stone House is open from June through September on Tuesdays and Thursdays from 2 p.m. to 4 p.m. Admission is free, but donations are welcome.

Essex

(Including Centerbrook and Ivoryton)

When it appeared that too many people were living in the area adjacent to the fort at Saybrook Point, settlement of some of the outlying areas of the Colony was encouraged. The Essex area was first settled in the mid-1600s and was called Potapaug until 1820. A degree of independence was granted the Essex settlers in 1732 when the community was named the Second Ecclesiastical Society of Saybrook. Essex was incorporated as an independent town in 1854.

As in many other river and coastal towns, shipbuilding was Essex's dominant industry. However, Essex held a special position among its sister towns: it was one of the most prolific builders and fitters on the coast. At one time, there were as many as 30 ships on the ways under construction. The *Oliver Cromwell,* built here and launched in 1775, carried 24 guns and is said to be the first man o'war owned by the government of the United States. In 1814, the British thought enough of the shipbuilding capacity of Essex to launch a major raid which destroyed more than 20 vessels. The largest ship built in Essex was the *Middletown* at 1,400 tons. The shipyards also served the builders of neighboring towns by providing sails and rigging for their newly-launched ships. In addition, Essex was a distribution point for much of the West Indies trade. Warehouses along the river were filled with rum, sugar, molasses, and tobacco for shipment in small boats to towns up the river as far as Springfield, or overland in horse-drawn carts.

One of the communities that is a part of Essex is Ivoryton, home of Pratt, Read and Company, the largest manufacturer of piano and organ keyboards in the world (for details, see Deep River). Another unique product of the town is witch hazel: the E. E. Dickinson Co., using a formula learned from the Indians, is America's largest producer and is headquartered in Essex.

Present-day Essex is one of the most charming towns in New England, with narrow streets and hundreds of antique homes. The beautiful harbor is a popular stopping place for cruising yachts. The charm, the harbor traffic and many fine small shops and excellent restaurants combine to make this a very busy place in the summer. The residents, now mostly upper-income retirees, probably grit their teeth at the coming of warm weather. But don't let that deter you; a visit to Essex village is a must.

Things to see & do

Walks and drives around Essex are well worth the time. Besides the lovely homes in the village area, the surrounding countryside and the communities of Ivoryton and Centerbrook should be seen. A fine map of the entire town pointing out sites of scenic or historic interest is available free at most of the stores and inns. An excellent walking map of Essex proper can be purchased for $1. If you're heading for Deep River or Chester from Essex, be sure to take River Road—very pretty.

The Valley Railroad — Train buffs, little old ladies, children, and just about everyone will enjoy a trip on the Valley Railroad. For just plain old-fashioned fun, you can't beat this 10-mile round trip with a roaring steam engine, a howling whistle, and the good old clackety-clack of long-gone railroad days. The coaches, most of them from the turn of the century, have seats that put Amtrak to shame, and a few of them even have wood-burning stoves. If you want to go first class, you can ride on the *Wallingford,* a plush Pullman coach from the 1920s that has swivel seats, wall-to-wall carpeting, and period music.

The train winds from Essex station along the Connecticut River to Chester. There are some fine views of the river as well as glimpses of marshland, heavy forests, and a few boatyards and marinas. The round trip takes about an hour.

But there's more! The train connects with several riverboats at the Deep River landing, and you can have your choice of a one-hour or a two-hour cruise on what is one of the prettiest sections of this majestic and historic river. At some point on any trip to this area, the Connecticut River should be enjoyed from the water, and this is the perfect opportunity. Excellent views of the hills that William Gillette loved so much, with a close-up view of his castle, the sloping woodlands, the town harbors and shipyards, and the beautiful waterfront homes all combine to make this a lovely ride. All boats connect with the train for the return to century-old Essex station.

To get to the station, take Exit 3 off Route 9 and follow the signs. The train and boat trips run daily from mid-June to Labor Day, and on weekends in May, September, and October. In December, there are special trains with Santa Claus on board. For schedules, call 203-767-0103. The fares: round-trip rail—Adults: $3, children under 12: $1.50; round-trip rail plus one-hour cruise—Adults: $5.50, children under 12: $3.25; round-trip rail plus two-hour cruise—Adults: $6.75, children under 12: $4.25. Infants (under 1) are admitted free on all rides.

Photo Courtesy of Valley Railroad

Valley Railroad

Essex

Pratt House — Maintained by the Society for the Preservation of New England Antiquities, the Pratt House has never been firmly dated, although experts have determined that at least part of it was built before 1690. With its hand-hewn oak and chestnut beams, featheredge sheathing, and narrow fielded paneling, this home is a fine example of Connecticut's mid-eighteenth century domestic architecture. The furnishings, mostly from the collection of Samuel Griswold, are from the 1700s and range from simple country to high-style Chippendale. There are especially fine collections of pewter, Connecticut slipware, and courting mirrors.

Located at 20 West Avenue, just west of the village area, the Pratt House is open from June 1 to September 30 on Tuesdays, Thursdays, and Sundays from 1 p.m. to 5 p.m. Admission is 50¢; children under 12 are free.

Steamboat Dock and Museum — Scheduled to open for the first time in the summer of 1979, the Steamboat Dock and Museum will be devoted to "the art, literature, and shipping memorabilia of the River area—a depository of the artifacts (documents, logs, photographs, paintings, etc.) which will graphically tell the story of the entire lower Connecticut River valley." Many of the items to be on display have been exhibited at the Hayden-Starkey Store and include, in addition to the above, nautical instruments, ship models, and maps. The new Museum also plans to have a working replica of America's first submarine, the *Turtle* (see Westbrook).

No better location could have been picked for this project. Essex was the most important shipbuilding center and port on the lower river, and the museum will be located right at the town's "front door," the place where sea captains and their ships arrived and debarked for over two centuries. The building, built in the 1860s, served as the steamboat freight and passenger terminal until 1931. The structure will have been completely renovated with several of the features of the original building being exhibits in themselves.

Funded by the Connecticut River Foundation, a private, nonprofit group, the Steamboat Dock and Museum promises to be one of the best and most important attractions in the area. The museum is located at the foot of Main Street on the harbor, and, as we go to press, its hours are still uncertain.

But if you're in Essex, be sure to check them out—it will be worth it. The museum complex will include the main dock building, a lovely park with a boardwalk along the river, and the Hayden-Starkey Store which will house the Thomas A. Stevens collection of maritime books and documents.

Ivoryton Playhouse — This summer theater, one of the oldest in Connecticut, has been attracting top names and large crowds for many years. Recent financial problems have left the future of the theater somewhat in doubt. For information, best call 203-767-0196 before you venture out. The theater is located on Main Street about one-half mile west of the Copper Beech Inn.

Dining

★Griswold Inn — In 1776, at exactly the same time that the Griswold Inn was under construction, Samuel Johnson, many thousands of miles away, was writing, "There is nothing which has yet been contrived by man by which so much happiness is produced as by a good tavern or inn." Johnson never visited the "Gris," but if he had, he would have been astounded at the accuracy of his own statement. This is one of the finest country inns in America, and is a "must" stop for anyone visiting Essex.

The building, the first three-story structure in Connecticut, is architecturally intact, though, over the years, several rooms have been added on to the rear. One of these, a one-room schoolhouse built in 1738, was hauled here and attached in the late 1800s; it now serves as the Tap Room, one of the greatest bars you'll ever see. Another room is constructed from an abandoned covered bridge from New Hampshire. Indeed, the whole place is filled with items garnered over two centuries of innkeeping. Beautifully integrated throughout the eating and drinking rooms are several important collections. One of these, an extensive group of Currier and Ives steamboat prints, is considered the most comprehensive collection of its kind in America. A fascinating collection of over 50 firearms (some of them more than 500 years old) is displayed in cases along the walls. Then there is the Antonio Jacobsen collection of

Photo By G. Allan Brown

Griswold Inn, Tap Room

marine oils and a wonderful bunch of steamboat memorabilia including bells, clocks, binnacles, and lights. Everywhere you turn in this magnificent place, another treasure appears. Architectural Digest thought so much of this inn, they not only included it in their *Classic Inns of New England,* they also chose to feature it on the cover.

But, best of all, the food complements the surroundings. The "Gris" describes its fare as "typically country. Our menu is printed in English. We call fish fish and beef beef." The menu changes seasonally, but there is always a generous selection of seafood, poultry, and a wide variety of various meats, every bit of it cooked with care from fresh ingredients. The baked stuffed shrimp ($8.95) and the lamb pie ($6.95) are particularly outstanding. The prime rib with rasped horseradish ($9.95) is well-known in the area, and one of the most popular dishes they serve. Whatever you eat here, you will have a fine meal at entree prices ranging from $5.75 to $9.95. Luncheon is equally good with a huge selection of sandwiches and entrees from $1.85 to $6.25. The Sunday Hunt Breakfast (served from noon to 2:30 p.m.) supposedly originated when the Briitsh occupied the inn for a spell during the War of 1812; it is a buffet feast of the first magnitude.

The Griswold Inn is located on Main Street in Essex village, about 100 yards from the water. It is open for lunch from noon to 2 p.m. and for dinner from 6 p.m. to 9 p.m. (10 p.m. on Friday and Saturday). Reservations are recommended. Credit cards: AE, BA/V, MC. 203-767-0991.

★**Gull Restaurant** — The Dauntless Shipyard on Essex harbor has had a colorful sailing and shipbuilding history for many years, but these days, the shipyard is writing a different kind of history: great food. The Gull, the only waterfront restaurant in lovely Essex, is co-owned and operated by a lady named Lu Lockwood, who has not only written a cookbook, but has had many of her recipes snapped up by Gourmet Magazine. The views of the harbor and the boats are terrific, but forget that—go here to eat.

The food here is like no other you've ever had and, with Lu and the chefs constantly experimenting and testing, the menu changes several times a year. Everything here is wonderful: the soups are super, the entrees enormously enjoyable, and the desserts delectable. A mystery roast (veal, beef, or pork) is served on Friday and Saturday nights and is invariably a treat for any gourmand. All of the veal dishes are excellent, and the special chicken dish (different every night) is very popular with the regulars as is the chicken prepared with peaches and bananas. Expensive? No way! You can have one of the finest and most unusual meals of your life for anywhere from $5.95 to $9.95. The luncheon menu features "salads" and "sandwiches," but again, like nothing you've ever had before, at prices from $1.75 to $4.50. If you're hungry, in love, weary, excited, depressed, or whatever, have a meal at the Gull—you'll never forget it.

The Gull is located at the north end of the Dauntless Shipyard which is found just off Pratt Street, the first street north of Main Street in Essex village. It is open for lunch from 11:30 a.m. to 3 p.m. Monday through Saturday, and from noon to 4 p.m. on Sunday. Dinner is served from 5:30 p.m. to 9:30 p.m. daily, but note that the restaurant is closed for dinner during the months of January, February, and March. Reservations are recommended. Credit cards: BA/V, MC. 203-767-0916.

Copper Beech Inn — The magnificent tree that stands in front of this distinguished inn gives the place its name and makes it a landmark. The Copper Beech is a first-class restaurant, and an expensive one: a couple will find it difficult to dine here with all the trimmings for less than $50. Happily, a dinner here is usually worth the price.

The setting is gracious, and the service attentive, but not impeccable: in our minds, there is a certain self-consciousness and pretentiousness about the dining experience at the Copper Beach that makes us unwilling to give them a star.

But the food itself, all cooked in a grand country French manner, is excellent. There is an exceptionally wide selection of appetizers, ranging from the simple to the elaborate. The entrees are varied, and those we have sampled were superb. Several entrees are called "specialties of the house," but in our experience you can't go wrong with anything. The dessert menu offers another staggering selection of treats, uniformly delicious. The wine list is a large one, with a good selection of medium to moderately expensive wines of distinction. They also have the legendary big numbers lying quietly in the cellar in case a Saudi oil sheikh, a Japanese transistor baron, or a New York show-off should wander up the Connecticut River valley. Before and after dinner drinks can be enjoyed in the Greenhouse Lounge, one of the most pleasant places we've ever been in.

In spite of our reservations, which are the result of the restaurant's taking itself too seriously, we concur with the majority opinion that places the Copper Beech near the top in any list of Connecticut restaurants.

The Copper Beech Inn is located on Main Street in Ivoryton, about five miles west of Essex village. Take Exit 3 from Route 9 and go west about one and one-half miles. Luncheon is served from noon to 2 p.m. Tuesday through Saturday. Dinner is served from 6 p.m. to 9 p.m. Tuesday through Thursday, from 6 p.m. to 10 p.m. on Friday and Saturday, and from 1 p.m. to 9 p.m. on Sunday. The restaurant is closed on Mondays. Reservations are a must. Credit cards: AE, BA/V, CB, DC, MC. 203-767-0330.

Old Saybrook

(Including Fenwick and Saybrook Point)

On Nov. 24, 1635, the Saybrook Colony became a formal settlement in the New World, thus making it one of the earliest English settlements in New England. The establishment of this community at the mouth of the Connecticut River occurred because of events that were taking place in England during the first third of the seventeenth century. Charles I had dissolved Parliament, alienated his own court, and was ruling the country with an iron hand. He was staunchly opposed by men like Oliver Cromwell, Hampden, Warwick, Viscount Saye and Sele, and Lord Brooke. Warwick had extensive holdings in the New World, and it was decided that a syndicate would be formed that would colonize part of this land to serve as a refuge for the noblemen should the opposition to Charles go awry.

The Saybrook Company was thus formed, and was to be headed by Viscount Saye and Sele and Lord Brooke. John Winthrop, son of the Governor of the Massachusetts Bay Colony, was engaged to establish the town and, upon his arrival, he hired Lt. Lion Gardiner, an English soldier and engineer, to build and command the fort. Saybrook became a military outpost and the first part of what was supposed to become a feudal colony of estates for the landed gentry. But, alas, Cromwell's forces were successful, Charles was beheaded, and the "gentlemen of quality" never arrived to settle their vast holdings.

Lion Gardiner, against many odds, built the fort at Saybrook Point, and settlement began. In 1639, George Fenwick, Esq., the only member of the Saybrook Company syndicate to come to the colony, arrived with his family. His wife, Lady Fenwick, came expecting to be the forerunner of an aristocratic society and must have been bitterly disappointed when the dream failed to materialize. She died in 1645 soon after the birth of her third child. Shortly thereafter, George Fenwick returned to England. Lady Fenwick's grave can be seen at the Cypress Cemetery on College Street; it is the only remnant of the early days.

The original colony was enormous, and contained what are now the towns of Lyme, East Lyme, Old Lyme, Chester, Westbrook, Essex, and Deep River. By the time the Colony had totally broken apart (by the early 1850s) the name Saybrook was left with what is now Deep River, and the original settlement that was the source of most of the early history of the lower Connecticut River was left with the name of Old Saybrook.

Today, because of its proximity to several superhighways, Old Saybrook may be the fastest-growing retail and light-industrial town on the Connecticut shore. The fort is gone and many of the old homes have been demolished; it is now very much a part of the twentieth century. But one should hope that the rich history of this town with the likes of Lion Gardiner and George Fenwick will not be forgotten.

Things to see & do

One of the most interesting drives in Old Saybrook is Route 154, which makes a big loop out to and along the shore. Take Main Street (Route 154) south to the William Hart House. In this area, there are some nice older homes and the historic Congregational Church. Just before reaching Saybrook Point, Cypress Cemetery will appear on the right. Lady Fenwick's grave can be found near the entrance and behind a small wrought iron fence. Nearby is a tablet marking the original commencement site of the Collegiate School, later Yale. A bit further down the road on the left is a statue of Lion Gardiner. At the Point itself, the Dock 'n Dine Restaurant sits on the approximate location of the original fort, and one can see how strategic a location it was.

Route 154 then swings to the west and crosses a long narrow bridge over South Cove. If you take the first left after the bridge, you'll come into Fenwick, an exclusive area of large old summer homes. Nestled against the Sound is the lovely Hepburn estate. Further along Route 154, the road follows the shore and provides some great views of the Sound and the tip of Long Island. Route 154 rejoins Route 1 about a mile west of your starting point.

Photo Courtesy of Connecticut Development Commission

Lion Gardiner Monument

General William Hart House — Now the headquarters of the Old Saybrook Historical Society, this beautiful home was built for William Hart in the 1760s. There is very little furniture in the house at the present time, but the Society is engaged in a program to acquire period furniture and furnishings. Even so, the interior construction of the house should be seen by anyone interested in early architecture. The paneling and molding and the corner fireplaces are very special, as is the "hardware," the latches and hinges. One hopes that the Society will persevere in its efforts to furnish the house, as this is one place that should be open to the public on a regular basis. A wonderful herb garden at the rear of the house features over 100 different cooking and medicinal herbs, all labeled.

Located on Main Street (Route 154) next door to the Con-

89

gregational Church, the Hart House has no regular open hours, but may be seen from time to time when there are special exhibits. As you drive by, check the door for an "open" sign— this place is worth the stop.

Dining

Castle Inn At Cornfield Point — This 38-room inn on Cornfield Point has a history as colorful as its structure is awesome. It was built in 1905 for George Jarvis Beach, heir to the Hartford Insurance fortune, as his private summer home. The original Tudor style mansion had 40 rooms and dominated 183 acres on beautiful Cornfield Point. The house and land were sold in 1921 to developers, who subdivided the estate into the summer community that now envelopes the inn. In 1923, a man by the name of Lindberg bought the structure and turned it into a fashionable hotel. Ye Castle Inn catered to the wealthy and provided not only a lovely retreat from New York, but illegal gambling and liquor. (During prohibition, the inn became the rumrunning center for this part of the state.) The present owners acquired the inn in 1976.

This impressive structure is situated on a point jutting into the Sound, and the two dining rooms have great views of the water and the boats, as well as the tip of Long Island and the Saybrook Point Lighthouse. The fare is mostly seafood along with a good selection of steaks and chops. There are daily Italian specials, which, as far as we are concerned, are the best thing on the menu. Their motto, "A fine kitchen is the basis of a good mood," is no bull—the ingredients are fresh and the preparation excellent. Dinners range in price from $6.50 for "catch of the day" to $9.50 for lamb chops or Steak Oscar. At lunch, you can choose from a variety of hearty taste treats (no sandwiches) from omelettes ($2.25) to a Mariner's Seafood Plate ($4.50). In addition, there are several main course salads. The Sunday Buffet Brunch (served from 11 a.m. to 2:30 p.m.) is regarded in the area as an experience not to be missed, but allow at least two hours to relax, eat, and enjoy. A variety of entertainment is offered Thursday through Sunday in the lounge. The good food, the setting, and the entertainment bring large crowds to the inn, especially in the summer, so try to make reservations during those months, and on weekends year-round.

The Castle Inn is located off Route 154 west of Fenwick and Saybrook Point. From Route 1, take Route 154 until you see their sign. Lunch is served from noon to 2:30 p.m. Monday through Saturday. Dinners are served from 5 p.m. to 9:30 p.m. Monday through Friday, and until 10:30 p.m. on Saturday. Credit cards: AE, BA/V, DC, MC. 203-388-4681.

Cuckoo's Nest — Can a family named Fitzpatrick from Pelham, New York, open a Mexican restaurant in Connecticut and survive? The answer, so far, is yes, and the popularity of the place seems to be growing. The walls are filled with the signatures of celebrities who have eaten here, and, while we don't doubt their authenticity, we wonder what they were doing in Old Saybrook.

The flavor of old Mexico is not apparent in the setting: an old barn surrounded by specialty shops. But once you step inside, amid the clay pots and plants in a small intimate dining room filled with the smells of exotic south-of-the-border cooking, you'll feel a lot better about coming here. The dinner selections are a full range of (what else?) Mexican food: every thing from the usual tacos and enchiladas to empanadas and great cheese burritos. For the uninitiated, the dishes are explained on the back of the menu, and, for the unimaginative, ground beef is available.

The Mexican food here is genuine and very, very good, but the prices will shock anyone from California or Texas. A single taco sells for $1.60, and three enchiladas with rice and beans are $5.95. The average menu price is about $5.25 and, while you won't fill yourself to the brim, you'll have a wonderful meal in one of the few legitimate Mexican restaurants around. A classical guitarist plays on Sunday evenings.

The Cuckoo's Nest is located on Route 1 about halfway between Old Saybrook and Westbrook and very near Exit 66 of I-95. Luncheon is served from noon to 2:30 p.m. Monday through Friday. Dinner is served from 5 p.m. to 9 p.m. Sunday through Thursday, and from 5 p.m. to 10 p.m. on Friday and Saturday. Reservations are not required. Credit cards: MC only. 203-399-9060.

Dock 'n Dine — The Dock 'n Dine Restaurant is found on Saybrook Point, the site of Fort Saybrook, one of the earliest settlements in New England. One look at the view up and down the Connecticut River will tell you why the settlers chose this spot for the defense of the lower valley and why many diners choose this place to eat. The views from the restaurant today are superb, complete with boats, birds, and an undeveloped opposite shore.

The popularity of this establishment can be measured by the tightly-packed tables and scurrying waitresses; an air of high-turnover efficiency pervades. The menu offerings include a wide variety of fish dishes plus the usual meat selections. Specials are the "catch of the day," escargots, and Coquilles St. Jacques which are all pretty good. The portions of most meals are large and filling. Entrees range from $5.50 to $10.95 with the very popular Fisherman's Platter of shrimp, scallops, clams, and sole going for $7.25. Children are welcome and have a variety of entrees from turkey to fried clams to choose among (about $3.75). And Sunday brunch is offered. There is entertainment every Friday and Saturday night in the Seagull Lounge. Dock 'n Dine is wonderful for a family getting off the road for a while, but if you're feeling romantic or looking for a fine, peaceful meal, head for Old Lyme or Essex.

To get there, take Route 154 from Route 1 and follow the signs to Saybrook Point; you can't miss it. (If you arrive after dark, just follow the flashing pink arrow.) Their hours are 11:30 a.m. to 9 p.m. on Tuesdays through Thursdays, 11:30 a.m. to 10 p.m. on Friday and Saturday, and 11:30 a.m. to 8 p.m. on Sunday. The restaurant is closed on Monday. Reservations are recommended. Credit cards: AE, BA/V, CB, DC, MC. 203-388-4665.

Westbrook

Once a part of the Oyster River Quarter of the Saybrook Colony, Westbrook gained its first measure of independence in 1724 when it became the Third Ecclesiastical Society of Saybrook. In 1840, Westbrook (from West Saybrook) incorporated as an independent town. Shipbuilding was the primary industry for many years, and Westbrook yards provided many of the privateers that harassed the British fleets during the Revolution and the War of 1812. In the 1850s, the industry went into a sharp decline and Westbrook lost about a third of its population and most of its economy. The discovery of the shore as a resort area in the early twentieth century went a long way to help in the recovery of the town.

Westbrook's most famous citizen was David Bushnell, inventor of the submarine. Born in Westbrook in 1742, Bushnell early on showed a talent for mathematics and invention, and became captivated by the idea that explosives could be detonated on or under water. After proving that the feat was indeed possible, he designed and built the first submarine. Called the *Turtle* (because it looked like one), this ship was first put into action in 1776 an an attempt to sink Admiral Howe's flagship *Eagle* which was moored in New York harbor. The *Turtle* was equipped with a boring device that allowed for the attachment of the explosive to the hull of any wooden ship. Unfortunately, the *Eagle* had a metal-covered hull, and after a night of frantic boring in the tiny submarine, the attempt was abandoned. Bushnell was also the inventor of submarine mines. During the Revolution, in New London harbor and again in the Delaware River off Philadelphia, he attempted to float kegs filled with gunpowder down the tide to blow up the British frigates. Bad currents, ice floes and whatall spoiled these attempts as well. Interest in the submarine and the mines remained high, but a discouraged Bushnell moved to Georgia, changed his name to David Bush, and lived out his life as a teacher and physician. In 1915, the U.S. Government named a submarine tender after this sensitive and brilliant man.

Things to see & do

Across from the Congregational Church on Route 1 is a beautiful old cemetery. A walk through here will reveal many interesting late eighteenth and early nineteenth century headstones. The Town Hall across the street is a renovated summer home and a good example of old-fashioned Yankee ingenuity. The harbor at Westbrook probably has more pleasure boats moored than any other Connecticut port outside of Stamford. If ogling boats and dreaming about Tahiti is your thing, a stroll through either of the Pilot Point marinas might be for you.

Westbrook Historical Society Museum — When Westbrook opened its new library in the fall of 1978, the Historical Society took over the old Public Library on the little green on Route 1 in the center of town. They have created a small museum and filled it with early items from the town. There are many old documents and ledgers and a fine collection of early postcards of the area. In addition, there are several interesting old maps. The Society plans to expand the collection in coming years. The building is open during the summer months from 2 p.m. to 4 p.m. on weekends. Admission is free.

Clinton

Until 1838, Clinton (named for De Witt Clinton) was the southern part of the town of Killingworth (see Killingworth). Since most of the early doings of the then much larger town were concentrated in the section closer to the shore, Clinton was the richest in history and commerce.

There were two remarkable men involved in Clinton's colonial history. Abraham Pierson, a Congregational minister, was named the first rector of the Collegiate School, a school formed by charter in 1701 "for the founding, suitably endowing and ordering a Collegiate School within His Majesty's Colony of Connecticut." The School was to be located in Saybrook, but the parishioners would not let Pierson leave town so the classes were held at the parsonage in Clinton. The commencements, though, were held in Saybrook. In 1716, the Collegiate School was moved to New Haven. It later was renamed Yale University.

The second gentleman was Jared Eliot, a student of Pierson who was called to the ministry following the death of Pierson in 1708. Eliot served for 56 years and had a remarkable career as a minister, philosopher, doctor, and scientist. It is said that he delivered more than 4000 sermons in his lifetime. He became one of the best known physicians in New England, and his advice and service were in demand from Boston to New York. Eliot wrote many treatises on farming and animals, and in 1762 he won a medal from the Royal Society in London for an essay entitled "Invention or Art of Making Very Good, If Not the Best Iron, from Black Sea Sand" (a sand then abundant along the coast). He was a close friend of Benjamin Franklin, who was a frequent visitor at Eliot's home.

Fishing and shipping played a large part in the development of colonial Clinton. As in many other Connecticut ports, an extensive shipping trade was carried out with the West Indies. Among the many products shipped there from Clinton was shad from the Hammonasset River, salted down and packed in barrels to serve as food for slaves. Today, fishing is still a part of the town's economy, but the manufacture of plastics, cosmetics, and small boats are the chief industries.

Things to see & do

An excellent example of the early one-room schoolhouse (this one built in 1800) can be found by going north on Route 81 and turning left on Walnut Hill Road (about one quarter mile past the High School). Follow the road to the top of the hill: the school is on a small green at the intersection of Airline Road. One hopes that the Clinton Historical Society will some-day open this fine little building for public viewing. Near the Old Red Schoolhouse is the Stevens Homestead, the oldest house in town (c. 1687), which has been occupied by the Stevens family for eight generations.

Waterside Lane (south of Route 1 just east of the Stanton House) leads towards the Sound. It shows that life along the Connecticut shore has not always been as peaceful as it is today. On the right you'll pass "The Arsenal" which, by tradi-tion, is linked with a fortification built in 1675. At the foot of the lane is a carronade that was captured by John Paul Jones and which found its way to Clinton by a long and strange route (read the plaque). At any rate, it was used to help repel the British invasion during the War of 1812. There is a nice view of the Sound from this site.

On a small green on Route 1 south of the Stanton House is the Gideon Kelsey cannon, which is being completely refur-bished and is scheduled to be rededicated on Memorial Day, 1979. Kelsey manned this cannon in a one-man defense of the town during the War of 1812. If you are still around in 2976, you might want to come to this green for the unwrapping of a time capsule that's buried there.

If the children are getting a little rambunctious as you pass through Clinton, there are several nice stocks in the yard adjoining the tourist information bureau (Route 1—town center). **Stanton House** — Located on Route 1 east of the center of town, this handsome house, built in 1789 by Adam Stanton, was left by his grandson Lewis Stanton "as a museum and art rooms for the education of the public, who shall be admitted free . . . ." Lewis, who died in 1916, also endowed the project, and the house is maintained today by the Hartford National Bank and Trust Co., the trustee of Lewis Stanton's will.

And what a museum it is! The east wing of the house is a general store that operated between 1804 and 1864. Everything is there from the accounting ledgers to the merchandise. The rest of the house is more formal and is filled with rare and valuable examples of colonial furnishings and fixtures. Among some of the prizes to be seen are an eight-foot fireplace in the kitchen, a cupboard reportedly made in 1670, partitions between two of the rooms that could be hung from the ceiling to divide an enormous common room, some fine Kensington embroideries, and a Georgian highboy that will make any antique lover drool. The parlor has the original French wallpaper hung by Mary Stanton in 1825. In addition, there are fine collections of Staffordshire, lustre and sprig ware, and quite a few interesting early weapons.

The real beauty of the house is that it is arranged as if the Stantons had just stepped out for a stroll; everything is in its place, and there is very little hidden behind glass or secured in cases. For this reason, every visitor is taken on a guided tour and, for the person who wants to see what gracious colonial living was all about, this is the place to go.

The house is open daily (except Mondays) from May 1 to October 31, from 2 p.m. to 5 p.m. Admission is free.

William Stanton Andrews Memorial Town Hall — You may pass this imposing brick and marble building on Route 1 thinking that one of the big insurance companies has set up an outpost, but a brief visit could be very rewarding. The brass drinking fountains alone are worth the stop. Given to the town by Mr. Andrews in the 1930s, this interesting building contains the town offices, a municipal auditorium, and a room specifically built for and maintained by the Clinton Historical Society. The room is constructed in the true colonial manner, with large hand-hewn beams and a huge fireplace. There are many displays of early documents, antique dolls, tools, and other items concerned with the early settlement of the town.

The room is open from 2 p.m. to 4 p.m. during the summer months; other times by appointment (see the Town Clerk). Admission is free.

Dining

Top of the Dock — This is a popular seafood restaurant located right on Clinton Harbor. Views of the docks and the harbor abound, but while the setting is nice, the interior decor of this establishment is fairly ordinary and somewhat less than stimulating. The popularity of this place stems from a broad menu of well-cooked food: there's something for everyone here.

While seafood is the dominant item on the menu (over 15 dishes to choose from), there are a variety of beef, veal, and poultry dishes available. The Seafood Top of the Dock ($10.50), a mixture of various shellfish sauteed in a clam and lobster sauce and served over linguini is excellent, as is another specialty, Veal Top of the Dock ($8.50). Indeed, almost everything you order here is good, and chances are you will not be disappointed. Dinner entree prices range from $5.95 to $10.50 (average about $8.00) which includes salad and a choice of potato. The luncheon menu is equally broad and features everything you can imagine from $1.95 to $4.50. Try the seafood crepe—very good.

To get there, turn south from Route 1 at any of the "harbor marina" signs seen just west of the downtown area. The restaurant will be found at the foot of the street, right on the water. Top of the Dock is open from 11 a.m. to 1 a.m. daily. Reservations are recommended, especially in the summer. Credit cards: AE, BA/V, MC. 203-669-7808.

Killingworth

By 1660 the New Haven Colony had established an eastern border with Guilford at the Hammonasset River. Saybrook, in the Connecticut Colony, went as far west as the Menunketesick River. Between the two settlements was an area of about 50 square miles unclaimed by the white man. During May, 1662, a John Clow, Jr. petitioned the General Court in Hartford to establish a settlement in the area and to call it Homonoscitt. The Court appointed a committee of three "to view the lands" and they reported that the area "will make a comfortable plantation for the entertainment of thirty families." We don't know what kind of entertainment they had in mind, but it must have been lavish: the plantation was to consist of 32,614 acres!

By 1665, settlement had begun. On May 9, 1667, the Court of Election in Hartford ordered "that ye town of Homonoscitt shall for ye future be named Kenilworth," a name most likely selected because it was the birthplace in England of Edward Griswold, deacon of the church, and the town's first delegate to the General Court. There is much evidence that the terrible spelling and pronunciation of the period soon corrupted the name to Killingworth.

Killingworth was the home of the famous goldsmith and inventive genius Abel Buell, who is credited with making the first font of type in the colonies and engraving the first map of America. He was a clever and skillful man who ran afoul of the law when his neighbors caught him counterfeiting five-pound notes. Shortly after being imprisoned for this offense, he invented the first lapidary machine in America, made a gold ring which he sent to the King's attorney, and was soon released.

As in the case of Madison, the settlement was too large to allow convenient access to church services and meetings. In addition, the northern section of town was becoming primarily an agricultural community, while the southern area turned its attention more and more to the sea: fishing, shipping, and related commerce. In 1730, the town was divided into two Parishes, and a church was established in the Northern Parish in 1737. By the end of the eighteenth century, it was obvious that the two Parishes should split into two separate towns. It is interesting to note that when the town was finally divided in 1838, the northern, less populated section retained the name of Killingworth, all the town records, and two seats in the General Assembly!

Today, Killingworth is an area of widely scattered farms and dense woods; those who live there now enjoy rural Connecticut at its best.

Things to see & do

Drives through Killingworth will be rewarded with occasional glimpses of some eighteenth and early nineteenth century homes and cottages. On Route 81 about one half mile north of the traffic circle at Route 80 is the Congregational Church. Built in 1820, this fine building is an excellent example of late Federal architecture and should be viewed both inside and out.

Chatfield Hollow State Park — If you get too much sun at the Hammonasset beach you might want to head over to this shady and beautifully maintained park. Stately pines and large hardwoods line the roads and surround the picnic areas. There is fishing in the central lake, Schreeder Pond, as well as excellent swimming facilities. There are fine picnic areas around the lake and along a stream to the west, which flows from a small pond with a working water wheel. An extensive blazed trail system throughout the 356-acre park provides hikers and cross-country skiers a chance "to get away from it all." The park may be reached by going west on Route 80 after the intersection with Route 81.

Madison

(Including North Madison and Rockland)

Until 1826, Madison was a part of Guilford and their early histories are closely intertwined (see Guilford). The land that constitutes the present boundaries of Madison was acquired in two sections by Rev. Henry Whitfield. The first section, from the East River to Tuxis Pond, was purchased on Sept. 20, 1641, from Wequash, a Pequot sachem, for "a frieze coat, a blanket, an Indian coat, one faddom Dutchman's coat, and a faddom of wampum." Three months later Uncas, the Mohegan chief who was later to become a good friend of the white settlers, claimed that the land was his by inheritance and the planters had to pay for the land all over again.

The second section, the land between Tuxis Pond and the Hammonasset River, was purchased by George Fenwick of Saybrook, who donated the tract to the Guilford planters in 1650. The combined sections to the east of the East River were to become East Guilford (Madison) and records indicate that by 1695 there were about thirty families living in the area. The trip from this eastern section of Guilford to the main settlement for church services and meetings proved to be long and arduous, especially in the winter, so in 1699 an application was made by the residents of the eastern section to form their own society. The application was finally approved in 1703 and by 1705 the first meeting house had been erected and the community of East Guilford was formally established. In the early nineteenth century, after having been a part of the larger town for many years, East Guilford petitioned to become an

101

entirely separate town and in May, 1826, the petition was granted. The new town was to be called Madison, in honor of the president.

Early industries in Madison included fishing and shipping. The fish, mainly porpoises and whitefish, were processed for oil and fertilizers. The smell from these enterprises is very much a part of the early records and histories. The important shipping business once counted as many as sixty "coasters" running the inland farm products down the coast to New York, but this industry went into a sharp decline when the first railroad was put through the town in 1851. The northern section of town, which was heavily forested, produced timber and charcoal. An extremely active shipbuilding industry came to a halt on June 2, 1890, when most of the yards were completely destroyed by fire. Shortly after this event, the outstanding shoreline was discovered by the "inlanders," and the growth of Madison as a summer colony was under way. Today, the town is primarily residential. With the appearance of the Jitney Players in July, 1923, Madison became known as the home of the first summer theater in America.

Photo Courtesy of Connecticut Development Commission

Congregational Church, Madison

Madison

Things to see & do

There are many elegant antique homes lining Route 1 in Madison, especially on the eastern outskirts of the downtown business area. At a small green just west of downtown on the same road is an imposing Congregational Church. The building, erected in 1838, is one of the finest examples of Greek Revival architecture in the area. East of the green is the original building of the Lee Academy, built in 1821. When the Madison Historical Society has sufficient funds, the school will be opened to the public; until then, the outside is well worth a look.

Photo Courtesy of Connecticut Development Commission

Allis-Bushnell House

Allis-Bushnell House — This home, located on the northern side of Route 1 east of the town center, serves as the headquarters of the Madison Historical Society. Originally built about 1785, rooms were added on over the years, with a final large addition in the 1860s. The furnishings, fine antiques for the most part, reflect the periods of the individual rooms and are well presented. Probably the most important object on display is the original petition to Guilford requesting the establishment of a separate community. Two new and unique rooms were set to be added on the second floor during the winter of 1978: an eighteenth century doctor's office complete with reference works, a pill-rolling table, and early instruments, and a child's room, with many fine dolls and toys of the time. The house also has an extensive library available for historical research. A carriage house to the rear has displays of looms, tools, and Indian artifacts.

The Allis-Bushnell House is open in the summer Wednesday through Saturday from noon to 4:30 p.m. In the winter, the house is open on Wednesday and Saturday from 1 p.m. to 4 p.m. Admission is free, but a donation is appreciated.

Hammonasset State Park — Sandy beaches are not all that common in New England, and beaches open to the public are even rarer. Hammonasset, with two and one-half miles of curving sand is the biggest, longest beach in Connecticut, and is very definitely open to everyone. The park is well-organized and maintained, and offers the visitor a fine opportunity to swim, eat, get a tan, or just sit back and enjoy Long Island Sound. Picnic facilities are everywhere, and excellent fishing can be enjoyed from a new jetty being built during the winter of 1978-79. For those fishermen who bring their own boats, there is a good launching site. Campers have more than 500 campsites to choose from, but reservations are recommended for the three major summer holiday weekends. Day visitors will pay a small parking fee and campers are required to pay a daily camping fee. Located just off Exit 62 of I-95, this park is a nice place to go whether you plan to stay for a day or a week.

Dining

★**Cafe LaFayette** — It seems somehow sinful to enjoy yourself so much in a church, for Cafe LaFayette occupies the first floor of what was once a Methodist Church built in 1839. There are three small dining rooms to choose from, and the whole atmosphere is quiet and low-key. This is a fine small restaurant with outstanding French food.

The dinner menu features about a dozen luscious French

entrees ranging from Canard Braise a l'orange to Escalope de Veau Trocadero. Prices range from $7.50 to $8.95 and include soup, salad, and a potato selection. If you want to share your meal, a fantastic rack of lamb is available for $20.50 as well as a Chateaubriand Grille for $19.95. But the finest meal in the house is the Steak au Poivre Flambe Bordelaise ($8.95), which is absolutely out of this world! Weekend specials include a lobster dish on Fridays and prime ribs on Saturday. The perfect way to complete your meal is with a cup of Irish coffee, a specialty of the house. At luncheon, you have a choice of sandwiches, salads, or entrees at $1.75 to $5. The Coquille St. Jacques and the Welsh rarebit are particularly recommended. Sinful or not, you'll thoroughly enjoy yourself at the Cafe LaFayette.

The restaurant is located on the north side of Boston Post Road (Route 1) right in the center of the business section of Madison. It's open for lunch from noon to 2 p.m. and dinner from 6 p.m. to 10 p.m. daily except Sunday. Reservations are recommended on weekends. Credit cards: AE, BA/V, DC, MC. 203-245-2380.

Woodlawn — If you're hungry and on a budget, the Woodlawn restaurant will be satisfying in both respects. Situated in a century-old building, this establishment, especially at lunch, gives you more food for less money than most of the good restaurants along the shore. The present owner has been associated with Woodlawn for more than 20 years, and takes a personal interest in each customer, a rare thing even in the finest places.

For anywhere from $6 to $9, you can have a choice of a healthy helping of fish, beef, or poultry along with a salad, potato, and two vegetables served family style. Their most popular dish is prime rib, available in two sizes. The house specialty is a two-pound lobster stuffed with shrimp, the cost of which varies according to the catch, but is usually about $15. Several Greek desserts are available, and should not be passed up. The real bargain here is luncheon, which has a selection of salads and sandwiches, most of which cost from $1.50 to $2.50 and include a choice of vegetable and potato.

Woodlawn is located on the Boston Post Road (Route 1) about one mile west of the business center of Madison. They are open from 11 a.m. to 3 p.m. and 5 p.m. to 10 p.m. daily. Reservations are recommended on Saturdays only. Credit cards: none accepted. 203-245-2616.

Photo Courtesy of Connecticut Development Commission

Thomas Griswold House (Guilford)

Guilford

In 1639, Rev. Henry Whitfield led a group of farmers from Surrey and Kent in England to settle in New England. On board ship the 25 men signed a covenant to "sit down and join ourselves together in one entire plantation, and to be helpful to each other in every common work." Because of Whitfield's friendship with some of the settlers in New Haven and Saybrook, it was decided that the settlement should be established somewhere close by. After arriving in New Haven, they started a search for a suitable location and in September, 1639, purchased from the Menunkatuck Indians the land from "Stony River" to the East River. The place was called Guilford after Guildford, the seat of Surrey County, England. In 1641, additional lands were added to the town and were to become East Guilford (see Madison).

Because most of the early settlers were farmers, agriculture was the primary industry during the early years. However, during the eighteenth century, because of the town's proximity to New Haven and the fact that it was on the main route between Boston and New York, a variety of small industries thrived, and the town grew rapidly. Quarrying became a major industry as well as milling and shipping. The granite base of the Statue of Liberty came from Guilford as well as the abutments of some of New York's major bridges. Present-day Guilford has many small industries but is primarily a residential town with many workers commuting to New Haven.

Guilford

Things to see & do

Of all the town greens in New England, Guilford's stands out as one of the best. Used for many years as a grazing ground for animals, a place where criminals were publicly whipped, and a training field for the militia, the green today is a beautifully maintained park that serves as the center jewel in one of Connecticut's prettiest towns.

Guilford probably has more surviving eighteenth-century homes for its size than any other town in New England. Many of these can be seen by walking any of the side streets surrounding the green. Of special interest is Fair Street (one block west of the green on Broad Street, turn right) with seven gracious eighteenth-century homes in a row. If you are a lover of antique houses and quiet streets, plan to spend some time in this interesting and lovely old town. A map showing every pre-Civil War house in town is available at the Hyland House for $2.

Hyland House — This historic dwelling was originally built in 1660 by George Hyland as a "two-over-two" house. A rear lean-to kitchen and attic were added in 1720. The furnishings for the most part are from the early 1700s although there are a few earlier items. It's interesting to note that many of the pieces of furniture on display were made right in Guilford. The stairway, also built in 1720, is a celebrated feature of the house. One of the most interesting elements found in this home is an entire wall made of the original handsplit clapboards from the 1660 house, which survived when the lean-to was added and the old outside wall became an inside wall. The attic is closed, but glimpses up the stairwells show the original beamwork and the upper sections of the huge chimney.

The house is on Boston Street, just east of the green. Maintained by the Dorothy Whitfield Historical Society, Hyland House is open daily from June 9 through September 9 from 10 a.m. to 4:30 p.m., and on weekends only from September 9 to October 1. Admission is $2 for those 14 and up; those younger are admitted free.

Griswold House — Now the headquarters of the Guilford Keeping Society, this house was built in 1735 by Thomas Gris-

108

wold and was occupied continuously by his descendants until 1958. After careful restoration, the house has emerged as an ,excellent example of mid-eighteenth century architecture. There are fine displays of the furnishings and fixtures of the day, but special note should be taken of the exceptional collections of quilts and napkin rings. The exposed bow back of a Guilford cupboard will be of a special interest to the antique buff. The "borning" room has a nice group of children's objects from the 1860s. A library is available to researchers by appointment.

The house is located on Boston Street east of the green and is marked by a prominent sign. It is open from June 15 to September 15 daily except Monday from 11 a.m. to 4 p.m. Admission is $1 for adults, under 12 free.

Photo Courtesy of Connecticut Development Commission

Henry Whitfield Museum (The Old Stone House)

Henry Whitfield Museum — This imposing home, a fine example of very early English domestic architecture, was built in 1639 by Rev. Henry Whitfield, the founder of Guilford. It is the oldest stone dwelling in New England. The building, known locally as "the Old Stone House," underwent a complete restoration in 1937, and has been maintained as a museum by the Connecticut Historical Commission. The furnishings are somewhat sparse but represent a fine collection of seventeenth and early eighteenth century pieces, the fireplaces and their fittings alone being worth the visit. This house served as the first church and meeting house for the settlers of the town; one can easily imagine the colonists gathered in these historic parlors. The grounds are pleasant and feature a fabulous herb garden.

Located on Old Whitfield Street south of the green, the museum is open from Wednesday through Sunday, 10 a.m. to 5 p.m. April 1 to October 31; 10 a.m. to 4 p.m. November 1 to March 31; closed December 15 to January 15. Admission is 50¢ for adults, 25¢ for youths 6 to 18.

William Pinchbeck, Inc. - The World's Largest Greenhouse — In 1979, Pinchbeck's celebrates its 50th year in business, and what a wonderful business it is. Here in what is (or, they suspect, was until recently) the world's largest greenhouse are 95,000 rose bushes producing over 3 million blooms per year, making Pinchbeck one of the nation's largest suppliers. The main greenhouse is almost a quarter mile long, and if you go in at the center entrance, it is quite a sight to look two football field lengths in either direction and see rose blossoms fading off into the distance. And oh, the smell! The tour will take you through the various greenhouses, the boiler rooms (and *you* think *you* have heating problems), the refrigerated "holding tank," and the room where the roses are sorted and graded. An interesting feature here is the Jamafa, a strange conveyor that sorts the flowers by size and shade. After you have seen the care and attention it takes to grow roses, you'll understand why they are so darned expensive.

There are no scheduled tours, but one can be arranged by calling ahead (203-453-2186), or you can take your chances and drop in between 8 a.m. and noon or 1 p.m. and 4 p.m., Monday through Thursday. Admission, of course, is free. The greenhouse is located at 929 Boston Post Road (Route 1). Just look for about 8 trillion panes of glass.

Westwoods Trail System — Every town in America should have one of these! Sponsored by the Guilford Conservation Commission, Westwoods is a 2,000-acre tract of wilderness that has been laid out with a system of trails now totalling more than 40 miles in length. There are marshes, ledges and trees of every variety. This is a real paradise for people who enjoy the woods. Every visitor should have a map of the area, which is available at the Town Hall on the east side of the green. The map shows details of the trail system and gives full descriptions of the various flora and fauna that will be encountered. The Conservation Commission, the cooperating agencies, and the private owners who have made this piece of wilderness available for the enjoyment of the public are to be congratulated.

The main entrance is located on Peddlers Road, west of the center of town. Other parking areas and entrance points can be located by referring to the Westwoods map. Admission is free, but a donation for the map would be appreciated.

Dining

Sachem Country House — Built in 1788 as a private residence, this handsome old building was designed by the famous colonial architect Frederick Kelly; it has housed a restaurant for over 35 years. A large, gracious lounge, done in a mixture of colonial and Southern styles, offers large drinks and warm comfort. The main dining room, large and airy, has walls covered with every kind of item you can imagine including paintings, decoys, antlers, plates, copper pots, and a great collection of antique pickle jars. Because the room is so big, the effect of all this stuff is rather pleasing and interesting. Several nice smaller dining rooms are available for private parties.

The menu is truly international and features Italian, French, American, and Middle Eastern dishes. The specialty of the house (and the most popular item) is prime rib, thickly cut and perfectly cooked. But we have also been pleased with the braised venison steak and the Coquille St. Jacques Mornay (both $8.75), and the lobster Newburg ($9.50). In fact, this broad menu has something for just about everyone. Entree prices range from $7.50 to $11. Luncheon selections include sandwiches, seafood, and beef, but be aware that everything is priced fairly high (average about $4.50). During the week, an excellent luncheon buffet is available for less than $5 and we would recommend that you try it in lieu of something off the menu. This is a popular restaurant offering a wide selection of different kinds of dishes.

The Sachem Country House is located on Goose Lane in Guilford, right at Exit 59 of I-95. The restaurant is open for luncheon from 11:30 a.m. to 3 p.m. Tuesday through Sunday, and for dinner from 5 p.m. to 9 p.m. Tuesday through Sunday, except it is open until 10 p.m. on Saturday nights. Reservations are recommended. Credit cards: AE, BA/V, DC, MC. 203-453-5261.

Chello Oyster House — The Chello Oyster House was first opened in 1936 and has retained not only the atmosphere of that time, but also the large portions that were in vogue during that period. Plenty of good food and fast, friendly service are Chello's trademarks. You can't mistake this place: just look for a mountain of clam and oyster shells towering in back of the building. The interior is directly from the '30s: formica tables, jammed-in booths, and large crowds. But you're here to eat, not look around, and you won't be disappointed.

The dinner menu features a wide variety of fresh fish and meat dishes. (Despite the fact that this is a "fish house," the prime rib special on Saturday night is extremely popular.) But if it's fish you want, there's plenty to choose from. The "catch of the day" is always excellent, as is the Seafood Platter, a mixture of fried fish, clams, shrimp, etc. If you're really hungry (and rich), the Shore Dinner is super; the double appetizer, two lobsters, potato, vegetable, and beverage costs about $15. Entree prices at Chello range from $6.75 to $9.

At lunch, you have a wide variety of meat, fish, and salad dishes to choose from as well as sandwiches. Prices run from $3.25 to $5.25. There is no lounge here, but drinks may be served at your table. Chello's has their own bakery, and are proud of their homemade bread and 7-inch "Sky High" lemon meringue pie.

The Chello Oyster House is found on Route 1 in Guilford, just about halfway between Exits 58 and 59 of I-95. The restaurant is closed on Tuesday, but on all other days it is open from 11 a.m. to 9 p.m. except on Sunday, when they close at 8 p.m. They do not accept reservations, but the wait is usually only 15 to 20 minutes. Credit cards: BA/V, MC. 203-453-2670.

Index

Abbott's Lobster in the Rough, 33
Allis-Bushnell House, 103
Amasa Day House, 71
Annual Ancient Muster of Fife and Drum Corps, 78

Bashan, 67
Bee and Thistle Inn, 62
Beebe-Philips House, 48
Black Hall, 57
Black Point, 51
Black Whale Restaurant, 55
Blessing of the Fleet, 10
Bluff Point Coastal Reserve, 32
Bride Brook, 52
Burnett's Corner, 27

Cafe LaFayette, 104
Cannon Square, Stonington, 8
Castle Inn at Cornfield Point, 90
Cedar Lake, 75
Center Groton, 27
Centerbrook, 79
Chart House Restaurant, 75
Chatfield Hollow State Park, 100
Chello Oyster House, 112
Chester, 73
Chester-Hadlyme Ferry, Chester, 74
Chester-Hadlyme Ferry, Lyme, 66
Chopping Block Restaurant, 55
Chuck's Steak House, Mystic, 25
Chuck's Steak House, New London, 43
Clinton, 95
Cockaponset State Forest, 75
Connecticut Arboretum, 36
Copper Beech Inn, 86
Crescent Beach, 51
Cuckoo's Nest Restaurant, 91
Cypress Cemetery, 88

Deep River, 77
Denison Homestead, 21
Denison Pequotsepos Nature Center, 20
Deshon-Allyn House, 38
Devil's Hopyard State Park, 71
Dock 'n Dine Restaurant, 92

East Haddam, 67
East Haddam Historical Society Museum, 71

East Lyme, 51
Ebenezer Avery House, 30
Esker Point, 33
Essex, 79
Essex, Walking Tour, 80

Fenwick, 87
Flanders, 51
Florence Griswold House, 58
Fort Griswold State Park, 28
Fort Trumbull, 36

Gelston House Restaurant, 72
General William Hart House, 89
Giant's Neck Beach, 51
Gideon Kelsey Cannon, 96
Gillette Castle State Park, 63
Goodspeed Opera House, 68
Grayline Bus Tour, 32
Great Island Wildlife Area, 58
Griswold House, 108
Griswold Inn, 83
Groton, 27
Groton Battle Monument, 28
Groton Long Point, 27
Guilford, 107
Guilford, Walking Tour, 108
Gull Restaurant, 85

Hadlyme, 63
Hamburg, 63
Hammonasset State Park, 104
Harborview Restaurant, 11
Harkness Memorial State Park, 46
Hempsted House, 41
Henry Whitfield Museum, 109
Huguenot House, 42
Hyland House, 108

Indian and Colonial Research Center, 21
Ivoryton, 79
Ivoryton Playhouse, 83

Jordan Schoolhouse, 48

Killingworth, 99

Laysville, 57
Lee Academy, 103
Little Boston School, 53
Little Haddam, 67
Lyman Allyn Museum, 37

Lyme, 63
Lyme Art Association, 59

Madison, 101
Memory Lane Doll Museum, 22
Millington, 67
Mischievous Carrot, 24
Monte Cristo Cottage, 48
Monument House, 29
Moodus, 67
Mystic, 13
Mystic Marinelife Aquarium, 16
Mystic Seaport, 14
Mystic, Walking Tour, 19

Nathan Hale Schoolhouse,
    East Haddam, 70
Nathan Hale Schoolhouse,
    New London, 40
Nehantic State Park, 66
New London, 35
New London County Courthouse,
    40
New London Ledge Lighthouse, 42
Niantic, 51
Noank, 27
Noank Museum, 32
North Lyme, 63
North Madison, 101
North Plain, 67
Norwich Pond, 66
Nut Museum, 60

Ocean Beach Park, 42
Old Lighthouse Museum, 9
Old Lyme, 57
Old Lyme Inn, 61
Old Meeting House, 74
Old Red Schoolhouse, 96
Old Saybrook, 87
Old Stone House, 109
Olde Mistick Village, 22
O'Neill Theater Center, 48

Pataconk Lake, 75
Pleasure Beach, 45
Poor Richard's Restaurant, 49
Poquonock Bridge, 27
Pratt House, 82
Pullman Museum, 10

Quaker Hill, 45

Rockland, 101
Rocky Neck State Park, 54
Romeo's Restuarant, 44

Sachem Country House, 111
St. Stephen's Bell, 70
Sandy's Restaurant, 12
Saybrook Point, 87
Seal Island, 18
Seamen's Inn, 24
"See the Submarines by Boat"
    Tour, 31
Shaw Mansion, 40
Smith-Harris House, 54
Stanton House, 97
Steak Loft Restaurant, 26
Steamboat Dock and Museum, 82
Stone House, 78
Stonington, 7
Stonington, Walking Tour, 8
Sound View, 57
South Lyme, 57
Submarine Forces Museum, 32
Submarine Memorial, 30

Tale of the Whale Museum, 39
Thames Science Center, 36
Thomas Lee House, 52
Top of the Dock Restaurant, 98

Uncas Lake, 66
United States Coast Guard
    Academy, 38
U.S.C.G.C. Eagle, 38
U.S. Naval Submarine Base, 32
U.S.S. Croaker, 30

Valley Railroad, 80

Waterford, 45
Westbrook, 93
Westbrook Historical Society
    Museum, 94
Whale Oil Row, 35
Whitehall Burying Ground, 20
Whitehall Mansion, 19
William Pinchbeck, Inc., 110
William Stanton Andrews
    Memorial Town Hall, 97
Winthrop, 77
Woodlawn Restaurant, 105
World's Largest Greenhouse, 110

Yankee Fisherman Restaurant, 34
Ye Ancientist Burial Ground, 38
Ye Old Town Mill, 39
Ye Olde Tavern, 43
Yesterday's Manner Restaurant, 23

114